The Poverty Trap

ISSUES FOR THE NINETIES

Volume 9

Editor

Craig Donnellan

First published by Independence
PO Box 295
Cambridge CB1 3XP

© Craig Donnellan 1995

British Library Cataloguing in Publication Data
The Poverty Trap – (Issues for the Nineties Series)
I. Donnellan, Craig II. Series
362.5

ISBN 1 872995 74 8

Printed in Great Britain
at Leicester Printers Ltd
Leicester

Typeset by
Martyn Lusher Artwork, Cambridge

Cover
The illustration on the front cover is by
Andrew Smith / Folio Collective.

CONTENTS

Introduction

The Poverty Trap is the ninth volume in the series: **Issues For The Nineties**. The aim of this series is to offer up-to-date information about important issues in our world.

The Poverty Trap explores poverty in the UK and around the world. The information comes from a wide variety of sources and includes:

Government reports and statistics
Newspaper reports and features
Magazine articles and surveys
Literature from lobby groups
and charitable organisations.

It is hoped that, as you read about the many aspects of the issues explored in this book, you will critically evaluate the information presented. It is important that you decide whether you are being presented with facts or opinions. Does the writer give a biased or an unbiased report? If an opinion is being expressed, do you agree with the writer?

The Poverty Trap offers a useful starting point for those who need convenient access to information about the many issues involved. However, it is only a starting point. At the back of the book is a list of organisations which you may want to contact for further information.

*****

Families, poverty and resources

Who are the poor and what are the consequences of living in poverty, in terms of resources?

There is great controversy over what poverty is, and how to measure it. Here we outline two commonly used measures of poverty, one based on how many people and families have less than half the national average income, and the other based on a poverty line (income support). Some of these measures only refer to individuals rather than families, but wherever possible we try to give figures for poverty in families. Different measures of poverty produce different numbers living in poverty, but the important finding is that no matter what measure is used, there has been a considerable increase in the number of families, households and individuals living in poverty since 1979[1].

How many living in poverty?

Poverty as under half average income
Using the idea of poverty being half of average income[2] – that is, less than £112 a week in 1990/91, at 1993 price levels – we find that:

- In 1990/91 there were 13.5 million people living in poverty (i.e. less than half the contemporary average income), which represents 24% of the population. This figure had risen from 4.8 million (9% of the population) since 1979, which means that 1 in 4 people were living in poverty in 1990/91.

- Children are more likely to be living in poverty than adults: whereas 1 in 4 of the adult population were living in poverty in 1990/91, the equivalent figure for children was nearly 1 in 3.

- There is a growing gap between rich and poor. From 1979 to 1990/91, the average income in real terms for the total population actually increased by 36%, but the corresponding income for the bottom 10% of the population fell by 14%.

A poverty line

Income Support is often regarded as a poverty line because it was designed as a 'safety net' for people out of work[1]. The number of people receiving Income Support in February 1993 was 5.5 million representing families comprising 8.8 million people[3]. In 1979, the number of people receiving Supplementary Benefit (the old name for this benefit) was just 2.8 million. The reasons for this increase are examined below, when we look at who are the poor.

Poverty in Europe

By comparison with other countries in the European Union, the most recent EU figures on poverty (defined as less than 50% of the national average household expenditure) show that, although four other countries had a worse rate than the UK, the UK had the highest rate of poverty among the more prosperous countries and, between 1980 and 1985, had the sharpest rise in poverty in the EU[4].

Figure 1 Official Figures and Unofficial Poverty	
Key facts in 1990/91	
adults in poverty	9.6 million
children in poverty	3.9 million
proportion of adults in poverty	1 in 4
proportion of children in poverty	1 in 3
Groups likely to be poor	
unemployed	7 in 10
lone parents	6 in 10
single pensioners	4.5 in 10
Large groups among the poor	
couples with children	4.9 million
pensioners	3.5 million
unemployed	2.1 million
couples with a full-time worker	1.5 million
Poverty lines = half national average income (£ weekly, 1993 prices)	
Half average income (per capita)	£112
single adult	£45
couple with no children	£82
couple with three children	£137

Source: HBAI, after Roll, 1992 (All figures are after housing costs)

Who are the poor?

There are two common ways of looking at poverty: according to family type, and to economic status.

Poverty by family type

In 1990/91 lone parents were at the greatest risk of poverty: 11% of the poor were lone parent families, whereas only 6% of the total population were lone parent families[2]. (See Figure 2.) The second most at risk were couples with children: 49% of the poor were couples with children, but only 38% of the total population were couples with children.

Poverty by economic status

The unemployed were at the greatest risk of poverty in 1990/91: 28% of the poor were unemployed, whereas 5% of the total population were unemployed[2]. (See Figure 3.) Different ethnic groups are affected by unemployment to different degrees: among black, Pakistani and Bangladeshi groups, between 1 in 4 and 1 in 5 of the economically active are unemployed compared to about 1 in 10 whites[5].

A large number of the poor are on low incomes, but not eligible for or not claiming Income Support. In 1989, a further 5.9 million families were living on income just above or below Income Support level[6]. As Figure 1 shows, there are 1.5 million families with a full-time worker who are among the poor. This is explained partly by the numbers of self-employed people who earn very little but are not entitled to claim Income Support or Family Credit because of the hours-of-work limit.

Families consisting of a disabled child or children are also at greater risk of poverty because the demands of caring for disabled children may make it impossible for parents to work: In 1989, 32% of parents of disabled children had no earners within the family unit, compared with 18% of the general population of parents [7].

The poor are not always the same people and families. For many people, poverty has a beginning and an ending, or they might be poor for several, short periods. But for others, poverty is long term. Recent research [8] claims that knowing how and why poverty ends would suggest the kind of effective policies required to address the different types of poverty.

Consequences of poverty: lack of resources

It is important to understand that being poor is not just a matter of lacking income, but lacking basic needs and resources. Some examples are given below but we are limited by the few national statistics on families according to housing, health, nutrition and education. Not having

People in poverty

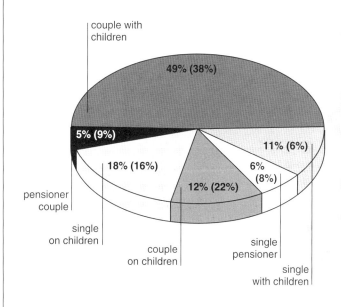

couple with children

49% (38%)

5% (9%)

18% (16%)

11% (6%)

6% (8%)

12% (22%)

pensioner couple

single on children

couple on children

single pensioner

single with children

Figure 2   People in poverty by family type

Percentages in brackets show the proportion of these family types in the total population
Source HBAI, 1993 (After housing costs)

Figure 3   People in poverty by economic status

(Percentages in brackets show the proportion of these economic groups in the total population)
Source: HBAI, 1993 (After housing costs)

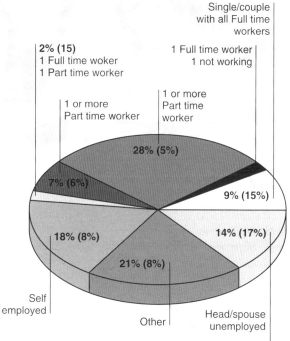

Single/couple with all Full time workers

2% (15)
1 Full time woker
1 Part time worker

1 Full time worker
1 not working

1 or more Part time worker

1 or more Part time worker

28% (5%)

7% (6%)

9% (15%)

18% (8%)

14% (17%)

21% (8%)

Self employed

Other

Head/spouse unemployed

access to a variety of resources means that poor families often live on the margins of society.

Income

It has been said that social security benefits, especially Income Support but also Family Credit (a benefit for families with children in low pay), are intended to act as a safety net, but is the amount enough to cover basic needs? A recent study by York University's Family Budget Unit[9] provides useful illustrations of what goods and services different amount of money could buy. Among the main findings:

- A low-cost budget for a couple with 2 children is £141.40 per week, excluding rent; yet, this budget is £36 more than the family would receive if they were unemployed and dependent on Income Support.

- For lone parents with two children, the low-cost budget is £110.41 per week; again, families on Income Support would have shortfall of £25.

Homelessness

In 1992, there were 140,000 households (about 400,000 people) officially registered as homeless, but estimates including the non-registered homeless suggest the true figure is closer to 2.0m. During the 1980s the number of homeless households with children rose by 46%[10].

Education

Education is linked to poverty because good educational qualifications improve employment opportunities and life chances. Yet in 1991, one in five 21 year olds was innumerate, and one in seven was illiterate.

References

[1] Roll, J 1992 *Understanding Poverty: A Guide to the Concepts and Measures*, Family Policy Studies Centre

[2] Department of Social Security, 1993, *Households Below Average Income: A Statistical Analysis 1979-1990/91*, HMSO

[3] Department of Social Security, 1993, *Social Security Statistics*, HMSO

[4] Child Poverty Action Group, 1993, *Poverty*, Spring

[5] *Social Trends 23*, 1993, CSO

[6] Institute for Fiscal Studies (forthcoming)

[7] OPCS, 1989, *Survey of Disability*, HMSO

[8] Ashworth K, Hil M, & Walker R, *Patterns of Childhood Poverty: New Challenges for Poverty*, Journal of Policy Analysis and Management

[9] Johnathan Bradshaw (ed), 1993, *Household Budgets and Living Standards*, Joseph Rowntree Foundation

[10] Commission on Social Justice, 1993, *The Justice Gap*, Institute for Public Policy Research

Written by Ann Condy, IYF Research/ Information Officer based at the Family Policy Studies Centre, sponsored by the Joseph Rowntree Foundation.

Family cost, income and poverty

In 1979, according to government figures, one in ten British children lived in households with less than half the average income. In 1995 this figure has risen to almost one in three. Deprivation varies between household types, ethnic groups and geographical areas. In Tower Hamlets, for example, nearly 46% of children live in households with no earner compared with the Ribble Valley at just over five per cent.

The public debate on poverty received renewed interest in 1994-1995. The publication of the *Commission on Social Justice Report* and *Social Trends*, the furore over salaries of some Chief Executives of privatised utilities and the findings of the Joseph Rowntree Foundation (JRF) Inquiry Group, all fuelled the larger debate about the increasing inequality in wealth. NCH Action For Children welcomed this debate

as it supports our concerns over the disastrous effects of poverty on children and families.

A helpful element in the debate has been discussion about the purpose of the social security system and examining the possibility of distributing existing resources to those in greatest need such as children and families as well as addressing the anomalies within the system such as

the poverty traps in which so many single parents find themselves.

The JRF report, published in February, found that income inequality in the UK grew rapidly between 1977 and 1990, reaching the highest level since World War II. It also showed that the pace at which inequality increased in the 1980s was faster in the UK than any other industrialised country, with the exception of New Zealand. The gap had dramatically widened between those dependent on benefits and those with earnings. Inequality grew, not only between different population groups, but also within them.

Government statistics highlight how the differences in income from work have grown rapidly. Particular groups and geographical areas have done disproportionately badly. Ethnic minority groups' incomes are well below the national average and parts of the country appear to be locked in a spiral of decline. The rising levels of unemployment amongst young school leavers and graduates continues to cause grave concern.

The Job-Seekers Allowance Bill, amalgamating Unemployment Benefit and Income Support, will come into effect in April 1996. Eligibility for the benefit will be more restricted. Rates paid to under 25s will be drastically cut, adversely affecting many young people struggling to live independently. As a result of these changes, the Government estimate that in the first year 90,000 claimants will lose all entitlement to benefit and 150,000 will have to switch to means tested benefits, often at reduced rates. This will dramatically affect many families with children, forcing them further into poverty.

Measures of poverty

Although there is no official definition of poverty, all the various measures indicate a very significant increase in poverty in Britain in the last decade. Among the different measures used are:

The EU Measure

By the European Union measure of poverty, which counts the proportion of households with income below half the average in each member state, the UK experienced the biggest increase between 1980 and 1985.

Opinion Polls

The TV series *Breadline Britain* commissioned surveys to discover what people considered to be essential items that everyone should be able to afford. Those lacking three or more of these necessities increased from 7.5 million in 1983 to 11 million in 1990, including 3 million children.

The 'safety net' benefit of Income support

The number of children in families on Income Support is 2,950,000, nearly one quarter of all children. This is three times the number of children (923,000) that were on Supplementary Benefit, the forerunner to Income Support in 1979.

Family budgets and benefit levels

The Family Budget Unit sets out a very detailed breakdown of the income required to achieve a 'modest, but adequate' standard of living for children. Compared with the child benefit level and two of the Income Support child personal allowances, there is a significant shortfall in benefit compared to the cost of bringing up children.

Households below average income

This is a relatively new series introduced by the government in 1989 to replace Low Income Family statistics, and has come to be seen as an important surrogate measure of poverty.

An analysis of the 'Households below average income' statistics carried out in 1994 demonstrates that since 1979 wealth inequalities in Britain have increased significantly.
- The richest 10 % have become 62% richer after housing costs.
- The better off 50% have become 50% richer after housing costs.
- The least well off 50% are only 10% better off.
- The poorest 20% are no better off.
- 4.1 million children in Britain, nearly 1 in 3 of the population live in families with incomes which are less than half average See EU Measure of poverty above). This number has grown from 3.9 million in 1991/2.
- The proportion of lone parents in the group of families with incomes which are below half the average has increased from 19% to 59%, and the proportion of two parents with children has trebled from 8% to 24% – 1 in 4 of all couples with children.

Sources: *Households below average income: a statistic analysis 1979 to 1991/2 DSS, For richer for poorer* by Goodman and Webb Institute for Fiscal Studies 1994.
- The above is an extract from *NCH Action for Children Factfile '95.*

Rises in real income between 1979 and 1992/93

(including the self-employed)

		Income before housing costs		Income after housing costs	
(bottom)	First	1%	−17%	First
	Second	8%	1%	Second
	Third	13%	6%	Third
	Fourth	17%	15%	Fourth
	Fifth	23%	24%	Fifth
	Sixth	28%	29%	Sixth
	Seventh	32%	34%	Seventh
	Eighth	40%	40%	Eighth
	Ninth	48%	48%	Ninth
(top)	Tenth	62%	62%	Tenth
	Total population	**37%**	**38%**	**Total population**

Households below average income survey
Department of Social Security

Groups vulnerable to poverty

A woman with two children taking 8 years break in total plus 12 years of part-time working has lifetime earnings of only 54% of those of a woman without children*

The focus of this article is on those families and individuals within families who are most vulnerable to poverty:

- women
- lone parents
- people with disabilities
- young people
- minority ethnic groups.

Their vulnerability stems from their restricted access to the labour market, thereby reducing income potential, and in the case of many women and lone parents, having the main responsibility of caring for children and the cost of bringing up children. Discrimination directly affects who is likely to be poor.

Families have a central role in society. They are responsible for the care and upbringing of children. It is therefore, of significant concern that families with children, both lone and two parent, have been hit hardest by the rise in poverty since 1979. This is despite there being an increasing percentage of families no longer dependent on a sole wage earner.

Gender can increase vulnerability to poverty. While the impact of increased poverty has been felt by all groups, within these groups women are more vulnerable to poverty. Gender divisions of labour in the household mean women generally have the main responsibility for childcare. Because of their domestic responsibilities and the lack of quality, affordable childcare, women workers with families tend to be concentrated in poorly paid, part-time work. For households where the male wage is low and where women are the sole provider, low pay is a major problem.

Disability can mean a greater risk of falling into poverty. Evidence from the Census and other sources suggests that families with an adult or child with disabilities have reduced access to employment. Living costs incurred by such families are much higher. For example, caring for a person with disabilities can cost more in terms of food, transport and heating. People with disabilities are made more vulnerable due to discrimination. This can take two forms: personal and institutional. For example, many employers doubt the ability of people with disabilities to do the job. Institutional discrimination can mean lack of access to some buildings and some forms of transport. The discrimination faced by people with disabilities combines to limit opportunities and to reduce earnings capacity.

Minority ethnic groups have a greater risk of poverty due to discrimination in the job market and wider society. While the minority ethnic population in Scotland is only just over 1 per cent of the population, figures from the 1991 Census suggest that people from minority ethnic groups suffer higher rates of unemployment and a greater likelihood of being in a low paid job than the rest of the population.

Young people, especially those aged between 16 and 18 years, have become increasingly vulnerable to poverty. The lack of employment opportunities, the failure of a guaranteed place on Youth Training, lower levels of benefit entitlements, and for those aged under 18 years the lack of benefit entitlement, have increased young people's vulnerability to poverty. This has occurred at a time when families have become less able to financially support young adults, so there is increasing evidence of their experience of severe hardship and vulnerability to homelessness.

* Heather Joshi quoted in Glendinning, C and Millar, J (Eds.) (1993) *Women and Poverty in Britain in the 1990s*, Harvester Wheatsheaf.

- The above is an extract from '*Child and family poverty in Scotland – the facts*' available from Save the Children. See page 39 for address details.

Back to the future

The Joseph Rowntree Foundation Inquiry into Income and Wealth, released in February, highlights the UK's growing income divide. Much of its evidence confirms and repeats the Low Pay Unit's contention that income in equality is greater now than in the 1980s when records began. Caroline Welch reviews the report

In highlighting the reasons why the gap between rich and poor has widened in the UK, the *Joseph Rowntree Foundation Inquiry into Income and Wealth* lends its considerable weight to those who call for the adoption of policies designed to reverse the trend of recent years. The inquiry was set up in 1993 to:

- consider evidence on living standards, incomes and personal wealth; and
- make recommendations where appropriate.

The findings, which confirm the Low Pay Unit's (LPU) own and those of many other organisations, have attracted widespread media support and are a damning indictment of current government policies which have been largely responsible for rising inequality.

The sheer quality and range of data drawn upon by the inquiry means the report and its conclusions cannot be ignored. Sources range from internationally accredited bodies such as the Organisation for Economic Co-operation and Development and Eurostat, to data compiled by various national governments, to university research from many different countries. The report concludes that:

- the gap between rich and poor has widened considerably since 1977, accelerating after 1980 and reversing an earlier trend to greater equality;
- differences in income from work have grown rapidly;
- particular groups have done disproportionately badly;
- the tax system has failed to slow growing inequalities; and
- social security is no longer making an impact on the growth of inequality.

Photo: Crispin Hughes/PhotoFusion

Some of the most vulnerable groups in society have fared particularly badly

In support of the LPU's own findings, the report notes that the lowest income groups have failed to gain any benefit from economic growth. Hourly wages for the lowest paid, for example have barely changed in real terms since 1978, and by 1992 were even lower than they were in 1975.

By contrast, median wages grew by 35 per cent and the earnings of those at the top by 50 per cent.

The report also confirms the LPU analysis of official DSS figures which shows that the real net incomes of the poorest households fell by 17 per cent (after housing costs) between 1979 and 1991/92.

A further important finding which supports the LPU's work concerns the growth of self-employment. Far from this being attributable to flourishing enterpreneurialism, the phenomenon is in fact contributing to the growing numbers on low incomes.

The truth is that, for many, self-employment is forced upon them by employers whose overall objective is to minimise costs and avoid any responsibility towards those they employ.

As the LPU has repeatedly pointed out, the rising pay gap is a direct consequence of such government policies as labour market deregulation and a form of 'flexibility' which is nothing more than acute insecurity at work.

This has been brought about through a series of institutional changes, for example, the steady dilution of workplace rights and the weakening of workplace representation.

In consequence, those at the top of their organisations have experienced a substantial increase in power which has in turn led to the huge leap in executive pay which is now the cause of so much public disquiet.

The problem of rising inequality has been made worse by the increasing numbers who are forced to rely on state benefits.

In the past, levels of benefit were linked to earnings. Since that link was broken as a result of government policy, the inevitable outcome has been that the gap between those reliant on benefits and others has widened.

A progressive system of taxation might have been able to exert an equalising effect on income maldistribution, but again, as a direct result of government policy changes which have shifted the burden from higher to lower and middle income groups, the UK taxation system is less and less effective in this regard.

Rather, it has a Robin-Hood-in-reverse effect, ratcheting up inequalities which already existed in pre-tax earnings.

The overall picture of wealth inequality shows how some of the most vulnerable groups in society have fared particularly badly; the low paid in employment, the poor in inner cities, certain ethnic minority groups, pensioners and others unfortunate enough to have to rely on benefits.

The outcome is that since 1977 the proportion of the population living on incomes of less than half the average has more than trebled, with 20 to 30 per cent gaining no benefit at all from economic growth.

In an analysis of the causes, the report points out that a range of forces have been at work – some beyond the reach of national government. Yet it is clear from the evidence that there is nothing inevitable about the UK's experience.

Indeed, income distribution data shows that in some countries earnings inequality actually reduced over the same period.

In five of 17 countries examined, the earnings gap actually narrowed, and in the 12 countries where it widened, the growth in inequality has been much smaller than in the UK.

The authors speak of the 'exceptional speed' with which inequality increased in the UK; only in New Zealand was the rise anything like as rapid.

The report emphasises the fact that increased inequality has not led to better economic performance.

In fact it goes further: it makes the important point that increased inequality is bad for all when up to 30 per cent of the population have no stake in economic performance.

The message of the inquiry cannot be lightly brushed off or rubbished in the manner which has become familiar when government ministers deal with criticism of their policies.

The members of the inquiry group were *not* drawn exclusively from sections of society who routinely criticise government policy and this adds further weight to its findings.

In fact, Michael Bett, deputy chairman of British Telecom, and Howard Davies, director-general of the Confederation of British Industry, are amongst those deploring the social divisiveness and economic waste. That should make uncomfortable reading for any supporters of recent policy prescriptions which have produced such an outcome.

A notable phrase from the report puts it thus: 'It is a measure of our common concern that we have in fact reached agreement on virtually all of the issues we discussed.'

Furthermore, the report notes that, far from national governments being in the grip of irresistible forces, there is scope for much to be done, given the political will.

Just as there is a multiplicity of causes, there is a variety of appropriate policy directions and these are contained in the report's recommendations.

They appear under various headings which include:

- education and training
- the labour market
- social security and benefits
- pensions
- taxation
- housing, and
- support for marginalised areas.

It is disappointing that it was not the unanimous opinion of all members of the inquiry that a national minimum wage be adopted.

Nevertheless, the Low Pay Unit welcomed the statement that poverty pay at work is no substitute for unemployment.

It is difficult to imagine a much more convincing case for the need for change than that presented by this authoritative report.

Even so, the signs have so far not been encouraging, judging by the dismissive comments issued by some within the government. All we can hope for is an end to the ideological tunnel vision which has guided policy direction for over a decade.

As the report states, such dramatic social and economic change leads to consequences which are even now probably not fully appreciated by policy makers or the population at large. The current lack of any 'feel-good factor' may be just the tip of the iceberg.

© *The New Review*
March / April 1995

Ministers launch drive to rebut Rowntree claim of growing inequality

By Michael White

The Government last night launched a concerted drive to dismiss the claim by the Rowntree Foundation that inequality in Britain has reached near-record levels by insisting that the take-home pay of the average British production worker is among the highest in western Europe.

After the Prime Minister had brushed aside as 'synthetic' Tony Blair's demands at question time for remedial action, the Social Security Secretary, Peter Lilley, made a detailed rebuttal of last week's Rowntree report during a Labour-initiated Commons debate.

'The simple fact is that since 1979 the vast majority have got significantly better off,' he told MPs, repeating the Government claim that rising numbers of self-employed 'can control the reporting of their incomes'.

Ministers are sensitive to the charge that economic and social divisions are widening, as evidenced by Mr Major's statement last week that he saw his job as seeking to reduce inequality. In a speech to the Commons press gallery yesterday, the shadow home secretary, Jack Straw, called it 'the most significant admission of his premiership', a concession Margaret Thatcher had never made in 11 years of 'brutal self-confidence' in power.

Yesterday, Mr Major and Mr Lilley insisted that all groups had benefited from what the Social Security Secretary said was a 36 per cent rise in average incomes since 1979 – more than the 31 per cent achieved in the previous 20 years. Pensioner income was up 50 per cent and even the income support safety net by 15 per cent. Amid angry exchanges with Donald Dewar, his Opposition counterpart, Mr Lilley insisted 'to define poverty purely as a fraction of average income is to distort the meaning of the word'.

> ## 'The simple fact is that since 1979 the vast majority have got significantly better off,' Peter Lilley told MPs

Mr Dewar's motion – defeated by 291 votes to 252 – urged action to tackle the caused of poverty and unemployment, including a welfare-to-work scheme and better training. He spoke bitterly of the widening life expectancy gap between poor and prosperous parts of Glasgow – as much as 10 years for men and seven for women – but was repeatedly challenged for details of what Labour would do and accused of embracing the Rowntree analysis without offering effective answers. Mr Lilley said Mr Dewar 'opposes almost everything we do but does not have the guts to promise to reverse it.'

Mr Lilley accused the Rowntree author, LSE don John Hills, of leftwing bias, and cited an OECD report which said that the net pay of the average production worker was 'higher in the UK than in all other EC countries except Luxembourg, Belgium and the former West Germany'.

Some Tory concern surfaced in the debate, with former education minister Alan Howarth warning colleagues against neglecting the balance between 'compassion and competition'. But another Tory MP suggested that poverty might be eased if the poor took up allotments. Toby Jessel (C. Twickenham) said 'They sit in front of the television for hours and hours on end . . .not growing their own vegetables when they could do so easily and cheaply.'

© The Guardian
February, 1995

Exposed: the myth of poverty today

By James Bartholomew

For the past few years, the British public has been misled. We have been told again and again that the poor are getting poorer. Labour has delighted in implying that it is all down to harsh and greedy Tory rule.

One report by the over-eager poverty lobby even suggested that the poor of today were worse off than in Dickens's time.

The whole fictional horror story has become accepted as though it were an obvious truth. Radio and television interviewers have taken to referring casually to the dramatic growth in 'inequalities of wealth', as though this was common knowledge and universally accepted.

Now, however, at long last, a piece of research has been published which brings out some of the considerable evidence to the contrary. Even this new research, by the Institute of Fiscal Studies, shies away from painting the full picture, but at least it has produced statistics which, one hopes, will finally silence the doom-mongers.

The researchers looked at those with the lowest 10 per cent of incomes, the people supposedly in the direst poverty. These are people, some of whom are apparently receiving income of nothing. And what did the researchers find? That these people, by some miracle, are spending as much money as everyone else.

Allow me to quote from the dry-as-dust text: 'In some years,' say the researchers, 'more than half of these very low income households are in the *top half* of spenders.' (My italics.)

Here is another remarkable statistic: the average spending of the poorest tenth (by income) has risen by 30 per cent since 1979.

Indeed, the poorest tenth of society increased their access to every kind of luxury during the Eighties.

The proportion with a telephone rose from 47 to 68 per cent. The number with central heating rose from 42 to 70 per cent. As for video recorders, which were still quite new in 1979, now half of the poorest tenth already has the use of them. This is not poverty as anyone from Bangladesh or Ethiopia would know it.

Among those who actually work, the rise in prosperity under Tory rule has been unmistakable. The least well-paid tenth of men have seen their real pay rise by a fifth. The least well-paid women have had a 28 per cent rise in real terms.

Even those most keen to believe in a worse-than-Dickensian Britain must surely be made to pause by these figures. How on earth can it be that those who are earning the very least are spending much more than in 1979 and, on average, about as much as everyone else?

Here we go out of the realms of statistics and into theories. The researchers offer the suggestion that, because there are more self-employed people among the poorest ten per cent, pensioners make up a smaller proportion of that group. They also suggest that the self-employed tend to have variable incomes, so they will carry on spending through the bad times in the hope of good times to come.

Such suggestions go some of the way to explaining what is going on. But they are not wholly convincing.

There are other possible explanations that anyone with any knowledge of the real world could easily make. In fact, a telephone call reveals that the researchers of this publication are well aware of these other possibilities but have discreetly chosen not to mention them.

One explanation is that the self-employed are uniquely well placed to make their incomes appear lower than they really are. They are better off than they appear to be. This possibility is made all the more plausible by the information (again not put into the published report) that builders were particularly common among those supposedly poverty-stricken self-employed people.

We all of us know, from personal experience, that builders are in a better position than most to camouflage their true incomes. They are often paid cash.

The electrician, the plumber or the odd-job man who comes to your home will often insist on cash or else demand a higher price. By taking his payment in cash, he is avoiding not only VAT but also income tax. He may even be claiming income support or invalidity benefit so he is, in theory, not in work.

A smattering of accountants, according to the report, is also among the self-employed people who claim to be making hardly any money at all. One can only smile indulgently at the naivety of researchers who have calmly included a platoon of qualified accountants among those suffering Victorian levels of poverty.

There may indeed be some unfortunate cases, but it does not take a cynic to think that part of the accountants' expertise is to declare the lowest possible income.

In short, the official income statistics cannot be trusted. Welfare benefits and taxation have encouraged people to conceal the truth.

The truth is that we get a far more reliable picture of people's wealth from examining what people spend. The figures on spending show that, at every level of wealth, from top to bottom, people have more money in their pockets than in 1979.

The poor are not getting poorer. They are getting richer. And this is happening despite major changes in our society which conspire against growing average wealth.

One of these changes is that the old are living longer. They have to rely on savings which are gradually run down and pensions which do not always hold their real value. It is a wonderful thing that people can now enjoy prolonged retirement, but inevitably their incomes in retirement are lower than when they were at work.

Meanwhile the welfare state has been sucking more and more people away from work and into dependency on the state. There has been a vast increase in the number of single mothers, who are often largely dependent on state support and badly off.

There has been a dramatic rise, too, in the numbers who are unemployed or discouraged from work by a combination of tax and benefits. These victims of the welfare state are likely to be short of money.

Yet despite these factors, the poor, as we have shown above, are – one must repeat – getting richer.

There may have been an increase in the difference between the incomes of the richest and the poorest but it is far less dramatic than has previously been claimed.

To some extent it has been highly desirable since, in 1979, the rich and the middle classes were taxed too much on their income. They had little incentive to work or to stay in this country. Now that has been put right and they work harder than ever before.

The Tory years have been a success in making most people richer – including the poorest. If there is a flaw in the record, it is not one which comes from the Tories being too capitalist and hard. On the contrary, it comes from the Tories being too willing to continue with the welfare state as designed by Labour.

The tax and benefits system has dragged too many people down. The Tories put right the incentives for the middle classes, but not those for the low-paid. If that anomaly could only be corrected, then all of British society could become considerably more prosperous.

© Daily Mail
May, 1995

UK accused of failing duty to poor

Britain's attitude to poverty and the UN social summit was attacked yesterday by charities and aid groups, as officials in Copenhagen struggled to reach agreement on the summit declaration due for signing on Sunday by about 120 heads of state.

Peter Townsend, president of the Child Poverty Action Group, accused the government of 'abdicating its responsibility to the poor'. He said that 'conditions among the poorest people in Britain are desperate and getting worse'. He added that ministers talked of 'low income' rather than poverty, and of variations in wealth rather than inequalities. 'We have to recognise humbly that we have to put right the problems in our own backyard if we are to acquire any authority to tell the Third World how they should behave in government.' He insisted deregulation, cuts and reduced taxation had increased poverty in Britain.

Baroness Chalker, Minister for Overseas Aid, expected in Copenhagen last night, rejected the accusations. She said: 'growth, which Britain is achieving better than for many years, is the only way to confront the problems of the poorest people.

'The United Kingdom, like all developed countries, has problems with the poorest, but it is nothing like the terrible deprivation in the developing world, which is the reason this social summit was called.'

But Timothy Wirth, of the US delegation, said the United States had to acknowledge its problems. 'There's no question about the fact that we have problems in our backyard with the environment, absolute poverty, illiteracy, teenage pregnancy and so on,' he said.

The World Development Movement, which took the Government to court over the Pergau dam, delivered a giant postcard to Downing Street, calling on John Major to approve action at the summit. It declared: 'In 1945, millions died because of silence. In 1995 millions will die because of silence.'

Officials at the summit agreed with Nigel Twose, international director of ActionAid, described as 'the most watered down version' of the 20/20 proposal, calling for 20 per cent of rich countries' aid to be spent on basic needs and matched by 20 per cent of developing countries' budgets. The arrangement, however, will be voluntary. Britain is refusing to back tougher wording favoured by EU countries and the US, but resisted by some developing countries.

Some observers fear the wording of the final document on debt cancellation, workers' rights and aid will be watered down. The developed countries want debt to be dealt with in bilateral discussions, and not in an overall agreement at the summit.

© The Independent
March, 1995

Family poverty

Working families and poverty – 'the poverty trap'

The workings of the benefits system itself mean that people can be only marginally better, and in some cases worse, off in work than on benefits, creating little incentive to find work and leaving people caught in a poverty trap. A major factor in creating the poverty trap is having to pay childcare costs in order to go out to work.

From 1st October 1994, under new legislation, low income families working and paying for childcare may be able to get up to £40 per week of their earnings disregarded when benefit is being calculated. It only applies to the following benefits: family credit, housing benefit, council tax benefit and disability working allowance. The disregard for childcare costs only applies to children under 11 and only under the following childcare arrangements:

- Registered childminders or nurseries.

- Registered out of school care run on school premises by school or voluntary group.

- Registered out of school care run by local authority.

- Childcare scheme on government property.

- Informal childcare arrangements with relatives or neighbours, the most common amongst low income families, are not included.

'I hate being poor. I hate having to sit in the same room, having to save up for weeks on end to be able to go out for a night. I hate having to say no to the weans. They're too young, they don't understand. I hate feeling inferior... it's depressing.' Parent, SCF project

The tables illustrate the workings of the poverty trap. The person on income support with a part-time job is worse off working, despite earnings of £60 per week. Even using the lowest childcare costs, the person is worse off by £20 per week – (she is ineligible for the new childcare disregard). The figures help to show that for many lone parents childcare costs are clearly a significant factor in deciding whether or not they are able to take up work opportunities.

● The above is an extract from '*Child and family poverty in Scotland – the facts*'.
© Glasgow Caledonian University, Child Poverty Resource Unit, Save the Children Scotland, 1995

Weekly income of a lone parent on income support UK 1994

Lone parent with one child aged 3 on income support	£ weekly income
Income support	60.15
Welfare foods	2.76
Child & one parent benefit	16.35
Housing benefit*	30.24
Council tax benefit*	6.85
Net income	116.35
Net income after housing costs	79.26

* The full costs of rent and council tax are met by benefits.

Weekly income of a lone parent on income support with part-time earnings and varying childcare costs (working less than 16 hours per week) UK 1994

Lone parent with one child aged 3		£ weekly income	
Part-time earnings			60.00
Tax			0.00
National insurance			1.44
Net pay			58.56
Income support			16.59
Welfare foods			2.76
Child & one parent benefit			16.35
Housing benefit			30.24
Council tax benefit			6.85
Net income			131.35
	Childcare	Travel	
Net income after housing travel and childcare costs	25.00	10.00	59.26
varying	40.00	10.00	44.26
	60.00	10.00	24.26

Source: Department of Social Security in answer to parliamentary question. Written answer in Hansard 31 March 1994 1029.

Suggestions for tackling poverty

Understanding the reality of poverty

- Ensure policies based on real understanding of present-day family structures.
- Enable people living in poverty to effect policy changes themselves by their participation in anti-poverty campaigns.
- Explain rights clearly, and honour them.
- Prioritise preventative family work rather than only giving help at a time of crisis.

Benefit and taxation system

- Increase benefits to realistic levels to allow for real costs of bringing up children.
- Make benefits available to all 16-19 year olds.
- Make the claiming of benefits, e.g. family credit, simpler for those moving in and out of work.

Day and child care

- Invest in good quality, affordable child care and nursery care.
- Provide day care for under-threes.
- Provide affordable day care in colleges and training institutes to enable adults to improve their futures.

Young people

- Develop better understanding of why young people are at particular risk of poverty.
- Ensure policies based on realistic assessment of families' ability/inability to support young people (lack of benefits for 16 and 17 year olds and low rates for older young people put enormous pressure on families).

Family life and parenting skills

- Prepare young people, in schools, for parenthood, the responsibilities of family life and the complexity of family relationships.
- Encourage young people and adults to acknowledge lifetime family commitments for elderly people as well as children.
- Set up family support services which recognise all parents need confidential support and which make asking for help a sign of responsible parenthood.

Single parents

- Becoming a lone parent, whatever the reason, rapidly heralds poverty.
- There should be comprehensive government policies, which do not discriminate against single parents, for all families.
- Lone parents increasingly have the dual responsibility of child care and that of their elderly family. Carers policies should recognise that many carers will be single parents.

Jobs and work

- TECs and employers should create opportunities for teenagers leaving school.
- There should be greater equality in the work place with better working conditions for women.
- Greater flexibility in working hours would enable carers and single parents to go out to work.

Education and training

- Help adults to return to education and training by introducing a comprehensive system of educational and training grants that make allowance for family responsibilities.

The departmentalisation of poverty

- Like family policy, poverty policies suffer because there is no co-ordination of government responses to it.
- Promote a government and inter-departmental commitment to invest in child care.
- Keep families together to deal with their problems, don't split them up because finding the funding is easier that way.

Equality

- Programmes to end discrimination in work and in access to education and training should be implemented.

Community support

- Give greater support to outreach work in the community through churches, youth clubs, voluntary organisations.
- Consider policies to enhance the quality of life for those whose lives are impoverished and isolated.

© Family Policy Studies Centre October, 1994

Where do you draw the poverty line?

Should Oxfam stick to working in the Third World, or does charity begin at home? John Barraclough talks to Audrey Bronstein about possible developments

Q *Why, after 50 years supporting development in other parts of the world, is Oxfam thinking of expanding its work in the UK and Ireland?*

A This issue has been discussed several times in Oxfam's history, but there are two main reasons why we are looking at a 'home' poverty programme again.

First, the people we work with in Southern countries are becoming more aware of poverty here. With the global impact of mass communications, and the fact that our partners are travelling more often, they're having more contact with the North. And they're amazed to find that the poverty they see in their own communities is also prominent in our society. They see homelessness and begging; people caught in the poverty trap, neither able to work nor able to have a decent standard of living on the benefit system. And they ask Oxfam what we're doing to help.

Oxfam has a small fund – £80,000 in 1993 – available to support programmes here, particularly work with the homeless in Oxfordshire. But our Southern partners are surprised to find we're not doing more. Second, it's clear that the gap between rich and poor is growing in the UK and Ireland. We felt we had a responsibility at least to investigate, to see if our skills and experience could help to reduce suffering.

Our Constitution allows us to do that. It states that our objective is to work for the relief of poverty, distress and suffering in any part of the world. At the same time, the economic policies that cause so much poverty in the Third World are being applied here.

Q *What evidence will Oxfam use to decide whether it should increase its work here?*

A Oxfam's Council decided we should look at the UK and Ireland as if they were any other places we were considering working in. So we commissioned a report from an independent consultant on the nature and depth of domestic poverty. We've also had discussions with voluntary organisations trying to resolve problems of poverty, homelessness and general disadvantage, to understand how they work. Then we can see if our experience and skills could be used to strengthen their efforts – which is the way Oxfam works.

Q *There are major implications if Oxfam were to start a home poverty programme. What would be the reasons for working here?*

A The idea touches a lot of nerves. But the arguments in favour stem from a very strong moral point of view; the feeling that we can't ignore our own communities. Many people feel that it would show tremendous courage and strength on the part of Oxfam, and would give us greater credibility in the South. They would see us tackling our own poverty as well as encouraging them to tackle their own. Another reason in favour is that we could use our experience/ and skills, and those of Southern organisations, to work closely with agencies here.

Q *And the reasons against?*

A The downside is more obvious, more immediate. Most people still identify Oxfam as a famine relief organisation, forgetting our support for long-term development. Working here might confuse people because there is no apparent famine on our streets. The public may stop understanding what Oxfam is about. They might not even want to continue to help, which would threaten our support.

There are also political implications. At the moment we lobby governments, the IMF and the World Bank, among others, on behalf of the poor. If we did comparable work here, it might be difficult to avoid the criticism of being politically aligned, although many UK and Irish agencies lobby and have very successful dialogue with government.

Q *Who will decide whether Oxfam works in the UK and Ireland, or not?*

A Oxfam's Council of Trustees will consider the issue and come to a decision in mid-1995.

Q *How can Oxfam supporters join the debate?*

A Many supporters have already contributed by engaging in forums and debates, and people have written to express opinions. There may be further forums, or people can write directly to Oxfam to express their views. They will be very welcome.

● Audrey Bronstein is leading the research which will inform Oxfam's decision on a home poverty programme. She is a former Oxfam Country Representative for Chile.
● The above is an extract from *Oxfam News*.

© Oxfam
Winter 1994/95

It's enough to make you sick...

Unemployment and poverty – it's enough to make you sick, say research studies which make clear links between hardship and family ill health. Save the Children's experience in the UK shows how poverty prevents children from having an equal start in life. . . .

A s soon as I saw them landscaping the river bank, I said that is the end of the shipyards.'

The unemployed of Pennywell estate, Sunderland – which has pockets of 70 per cent joblessness – are discussing the futures market. It's no more buoyant than the ghosts of ships in an area which once relied on shipbuilding and coal. As one young man said:

'It's not that people don't want to work, it's just there's nowt for them. I left school when I was 16. I'm 30 now and I have never had a job.'

It's a young population: 30 per cent of the 10,000 people on Pennywell are under 21. Parents worry that their kids will never find work. They worry, too, about the impact of low income on their children's health and growth; they just can't afford the right diet or provide a healthy environment. Women are prepared to go without to feed the children says health worker Elspeth Camm:

'They tend to skip breakfast, exist on sugary drinks all day and just have a meal at night.'

Now local people are taking action for better health through the Pennywell Neighbourhood Centre, run in partnership between Save the Children and the council. Before the centre was built in 1990, there were very limited health services on Pennywell.

By Lotte Hughes

Parents could not afford the bus fares to visit clinics two miles away. Now they sit on the management committee which organises services like the Well Woman Clinic, the Male Only Contraceptive Clinic (one of the first in the country) and treatment room.

Some statistics
Sunderland has the fourth highest number of smoking-related deaths in the UK. Low birthweights are common. High rates of respiratory disease and stress feature widely. Paul Woodhead, SCF's family work

development officer, sees everyday evidence that poverty-linked stress fractures families: 'We find a lot of kids will disappear for a while off the estate . . .and it's usually because of family tensions.'

Paul was sorry to see that the Government's Health of the Nation White Paper 'didn't mention income at all, in 130 pages'. Yet he sees mums like Heather, who can't pay the bus fares to take her five children – who variously suffer from epilepsy, chronic bronchitis and asthma – to the GP. 'I come here for Richard's injections,' says Heather of her youngest child, lucky to be alive after being born seriously underweight and premature. 'If I want something, I've only got to come and ask Elspeth.'

Families increasingly rely on women working part-time in local service industries – for £2 an hour. Together with long-term male unemployment this pattern of work is shifting childcare responsibilities over to the men.

Unemployed father of two, Kevin Craik, 29, says he enjoys bringing the baby to be weighed. He also approves of the Male Only Contraceptive Clinic and the men's group, run by Paul Woodhead:

'We sit and talk about stress, addiction – drugs and alcohol and all that – blood pressure and what to do about it. It's a friendly place to come if you want something explaining.'

Parents are well aware that health prevention is better than cure. 'People all know what they should do,' says Elspeth. But money problems undercut everything. 'I'm getting £123 a fortnight,' says Kevin Craik, 'and I'm paying two loans off. I tell you something: it does not go far! Money is my main problem.'

Being unemployed, low paid and under pressure makes people feel powerless to change things. As Paul Woodhead puts it: 'Poverty takes away people's ability to be assertive about their own health care.' That's why the work of the women's group to raise awareness and take action is vital for the whole family. The group has tackled subjects like healthy eating, stress, addiction, environmental health and child abuse.

'Since we've come to the centre, we've all opened our horizons,' says Sharon Dixon, mother of four and chair of the Pennywell management committee. 'The good thing about the men's and women's groups is you can come up with your own ideas,' says fellow committee member Carol Green, mother of Darren and Sarah.

New horizons

Both Elspeth Camm and family planning nurse Yvonne Batt welcomes this way of working. Elspeth explains: 'It's about being straight with people. But it's not so secure: people criticise and question what you are doing. I might have qualifications as a nurse, but people have skills that I haven't. I am often amazed by how well people do manage on the money. You can tap into their skills and they can tap into yours.'

Long term, Elspeth hopes that the accumulated trust will pay dividends as Pennywell's youth grows up. 'You may see a little girl you've known in the youth group who will be more likely to come and see you because she knows you. That's going to be a big plus. You can't work with anybody if they won't listen to you.'

SCF's contribution to Pennywell Neighbourhood Centre in 1993/4 was £55,318.

Where income support falls short

By Peter White

How much money is needed to bring up a child? What is the true 'poverty line'? These are hotly debated questions, with many complications and little overall agreement.

Now a new measure has been defined, not by professionals but by the real experts – mothers. The campaigning Child Poverty Action Group (CPAG) has published a new report presenting a minimum budget standard of essential items which has been drawn up and agreed by around two hundred mothers from different parts of the country and different socio-economic backgrounds.

They considered the things they regarded as the 'minimum essential' in the light of the United Nations Convention on the Rights of the Child: article 27 covers 'the right of every child to a standard of living adequate for the child's physical, mental, spiritual, moral and social development'.

All the mothers agreed that these amounts could not be reduced any further. Yet, for children under 11 they are on average £7.92 a week less than income support rates. For a boy aged from 2-5 the shortfall is as much as £11.75 a week.

The director of Child Poverty Action Group, Sally Witcher, said: 'The poverty line defined by mothers, who are surely the best placed to know, clearly reveals the inadequacy of income support. Children are suffering, both in terms of their exclusion from childhood society and because their basic needs cannot be met from inadequate benefit. 'The research is described in *Family Fortunes: pressures on parents and children in the 1990s*, by Sue Middleton, Karl Ashworth and Robert Walker, available, price £7.95 including postage, from CPAG, 1-5 Bath Street, London EC1V 9PY.

Parents' minimum essential budget standard (£ per week)				
Age	*Under 2*	*2-5*	*6-10*	*11-16*
Food	6.85	9.36	9.72	10.11
Clothes girl	5.57	7.13	6.94	5.83
boy	5.41	8.65	6.49	6.34
Possessions and equipment	4.75	3.13	2.20	4.13
Activities	1.75	7.53	7.45	7.36
Furniture and decorating	0.17	0.54	0.54	0.62
Laundry	0.86	0.86	0.62	0.62
Toiletries girl	6.54	2.18	0.65	2.45
boy	6.54	2.18	0.65	1.99
Total girl	**26.49**	**30.73**	**28.12**	**31.04**
boy	**26.33**	**32.25**	**27.67**	**31.09**

Child and family poverty in Scotland – the facts

One in three children in Scotland are living in poverty. Twenty five per cent of under 16s in Scotland live in households dependent on income support.

The purpose of this article is to provide detailed statistics on poverty and how it affects families, children and young people in Scotland. The collection of the following data was prompted by a lack of reliable and accessible statistics on the increase in child and family poverty in Scotland. The aim is both to highlight the increase and to provide those working or studying in the anti-poverty field with a range of useful information.

What is poverty?

Some commentators hold the view that poverty is simply about lacking the basics necessary for survival: absolute poverty. Absolute definitions of poverty work on the assumption that it is possible to define a minimum living standard based on 'a person's biological needs for food, water, clothing and shelter.'[1] Others take a wider analysis to include social exclusion: relative poverty. A relative definition of poverty goes beyond purely material needs and defines poverty in relation to 'the generally accepted standard of living in a specific society at a specific time.'[1] This article takes the view that poverty includes both material deprivation and social exclusion. People live in poverty when they are denied an income sufficient for their material needs and when these circumstances exclude them from taking part in activities which are an accepted part of daily life.

The UK has no official definition of a poverty line or minimum standard of living. In this it is out of step with the rest of the European Union. Whether measured by the

number of income support claimants or households below average income (HBAI), poverty in the UK has increased dramatically since 1979 and families with children and young people have experienced increasing vulnerability to poverty.

What has caused the rise in poverty?

Oppenheim[1] amongst others points to four main changes in society in the last 15 years which have led to a rise in poverty: rising unemployment, economic change, reductions in benefits and growing inequality. All four features are present in Scotland.

There has been an enormous increase in unemployment in the last decade and a half. Large-scale unemployment is now a fact of life for thousands of families in Scotland. Economic change producing a contraction in the traditional industries such as mining, ship-building and heavy engineering, has ended job and income security for thousands of Scottish workers and their families. These forms of

employment have been replaced by a rise in jobs in the service sector, an increase in part-time employment and a rise in self-employment, many of which have less security and lower wage levels, adding considerably to the rise in low pay in Scotland. The safety net provided by state benefits has been systematically eroded over the last 15 years. Not only does this include restrictions on entitlements but the relative value of benefits has declined. There has been a rise in inequality over the last decade and a half. Between 1979 and 92 the richest 10% of the income scale have seen their income increase by £87 per week. This is in contrast to the poorest 10% who, over the same period, have suffered a loss of £1 per week.[2]

These economic changes have gone hand in hand with demographic changes in family patterns which have made some groups more vulnerable to poverty. For example, there has been a rise in the number of households headed by a lone parent.

Lone parent families now comprise around 20% of all Scottish families. Over 70% of lone parents are dependent on income support because of the difficulties of taking up employment caused by lack of childcare facilities and high levels of unemployment.

What are the effects of poverty?

Poverty is not only about lack of income. Evidence suggests that it adversely affects health, education and access to housing. Poor people have higher mortality levels. Children born into poor households tend to have lower birth weights and have a greater chance of dying in infancy than their wealthier peers. In education, the effects of poverty are demonstrated when children from deprived areas leave school earlier and with fewer qualifications than their middle class counterparts. It is for these reasons that current statistics on the effects of deprivation on issues such as health, education and housing have been included.

The facts about poverty – summary of findings

The statistics on poverty are very varied and in carrying out our research we have drawn on many sources including the Benefits Agency and data from the health service and the Census. In order, however, for the reader to make best use of the data, we have divided it into the following sections.

Income and household resources

Income and household resources of those in poverty deals with statistics on family incomes, resources, costs and expenditure. Key points highlighted in this section are that:

- 25% of children and around 17% of the population in Scotland are now dependent on income support.
- 38% of under 18 year olds and 42% of under 5 year olds in Scotland are living in households with below 50% average incomes.
- Family credit claims rose by 21% between May 1992 and May 1993 reflecting an increase in families living on the margins of poverty. In 1993, 34% of children under 16 in Scotland were living in households in receipt of either family credit or income support.
- In 1992 housing, food and fuel/ light and power accounted for nearly 50% of the household budget for households living on less than £125 per week. The corresponding figure for households with incomes greater than £600 per week was 36%.

Employment, low pay and family poverty

Poverty is frequently a structural problem caused by high unemployment, low pay and the increase in insecure, part-time working. Key points highlighted in this section are that:

- Unemployment has soared in the last 15 years. Long-term unemployment amongst people aged 24-59 years old is increasing.
- 43% of Scotland's workers (both full- and part-time) are low paid according to the Scottish Low Pay Unit.
- Government policies are making some people poorer, for example, the imposition of VAT on fuel and the failure to maintain the value of state benefits, especially child benefit.
- Economic change – the decline of the heavy industrial sector and the rise in low paid, part-time working has pushed many families into poverty.

Groups vulnerable to poverty

Groups vulnerable to poverty concentrates on those people and families who are most at risk of poverty. Key points highlighted in this section are that:

- Women are much more likely to be poor than men. In 1993, 48% of Scottish full-time women-workers were on low pay compared to 20% of male full-time workers. 75% of women part-time workers are on low pay.
- 20% of all Scottish families are headed by a lone parent according to the 1991 Census. Over 90% are headed by a woman and around 70% of these families are dependent on income support.
- Large families are more likely to be poor. According to the 1991 Census nearly one-quarter of large families contain an unemployed adult compared to around 15% for one-child families. Large families are more likely to live in overcrowded accommodation.
- Only about 18% of adults of working age with disabilities in Scotland were in some form of employment according to the 1991 Census. Families with children or adults with disabilities have higher heating, food and transport costs and are therefore more vulnerable to poverty.
- Removal of benefit entitlements from young people since 1988 has driven many into poverty and

increased their vulnerability to homelessness. By 1993 claims for severe hardship payments had increased by more than 350% since their introduction in 1988.
- Figures from the 1991 Census show that there were higher unemployment levels in Scotland amongst people from minority ethnic communities.

Living with poverty

Deals with the effects of living in poverty. Lack of adequate income impacts on families in a number of ways. Key points highlighted in this section are that:

- In 1993 in the UK, 1 in 3 children from professional backgrounds obtained a degree. Only 1 in 30 from unskilled manual backgrounds obtained a degree.
- In 1991, mortality rates were 162% higher in the most deprived areas in Scotland than in the affluent areas.
- In 1993, the percentage of babies with a low birth weight was almost twice as high in the most deprived areas as in affluent areas.
- Poverty limits access to decent housing. Those who are unemployed are twice as likely to live in a damp house than those who are employed.
- The alarming rise in homelessness in recent years is yet another effect of the rise in poverty. Since 1979 there has been an increase of 177% in the number of households applying to local authorities as homeless.
- Children from poorer backgrounds are more likely to be taken into care. Strathclyde figures show that 78% of children coming into care between 1985 and 1992 were from families relying on benefits. Children who have been in care are also more vulnerable to homelessness.

[1] Oppenheim, C (1993), *Poverty: The Facts*, Child Poverty Action Group
[2] Davies et al quoted in Oppenheim (1993)
- The above is an extract from *Child and family poverty in Scotland – the facts*.

© Glasgow Caledonian University Child Poverty Resource Unit Save the Children Scotland, 1995

Poverty is a war against children

Information from Save the Children Northern Ireland

What is poverty?

Poverty is difficult to define. At one end, it can mean homelessness and destruction. For others, it can mean a home they can't afford, a family they can't support and basic needs they can't fulfill. But for all people surviving in difficult circumstances the territory of the poor has more common ground than difference. And with all kinds of poverty, children are always the most vulnerable.

In Northern Ireland, a staggering 30% of people live in poverty. That means, for one in three people, poverty is not having a decent winter coat or not being able to afford to go to the cinema. Poverty is a daily battle against deprivation. It's about not having enough to eat, or the right kind of food to eat. It's about the pain and stress of always having to say no to your children. It's about being deprived of your physical, social, and emotional needs. It means exclusion, powerlessness and indignity. It means anger. And inevitably, poverty untackled, means more poverty.

The causes of child poverty

Northern Ireland's endemic poverty has not happened by accident. Many factors have combined to cause what is now an urgent social and political problem. Some causes fit a Europe-wide pattern and others are unique to Northern Ireland.

Unemployment

Unemployment is the major cause of poverty. Northern Ireland has the highest level of unemployment compared to any area in Britain. It also has the highest level of unemployment in Europe. The current unemployment rate stands at 12.4% of the population, that's over 92,000 people without work. The unemployed rely either on unemployment benefit or income support, both of which have been cut in real terms over the last fifteen years. The reality for most unemployed people now is a life fighting a constant battle against poverty.

Low wages and changing employment

The poverty of 'employment on low wages' is often a hidden factor in the poverty debate. Sadly, the term 'the working poor' is fast becoming a social norm. Earnings in Northern Ireland have always been lower than those in the UK. Changing employment practices have not helped either. The number of part-time and low-paid employees increased by over 10% during the 1980s – most of these jobs being taken by women.

Inadequate benefits

In a decade of deepening recession and spiralling unemployment, access to state support has been substantially reduced. Families and children have been hurt most. Changes to eligibility for benefit have greatly affected the level of state support to families. A significant number of benefits have not been uprated and have certainly not kept in line with inflation. This means that, in real terms, they are worth substantially less than they were ten years ago.

Who are most affected?

Children

An estimated 37% of our children – 137,000 – are affected by poverty. Benefit levels fail miserably to meet the needs of families and children who are dependent on them. The circumstances of the key groups who are most at risk from, or who suffer because of poverty – unemployed, the elderly, families with children, lone parents, people with disabilities – all can have damaging implications for children.

Families with children and lone parent families

Families are more susceptible to poverty now because of higher levels of unemployment and the growth in lone parent families. There are some 50,000 lone parent families, with 96,000 children in Northern Ireland. 66,000 of these children are dependent on benefit.

Many lone parent families have found that the major barrier to returning to work is the lack of adequate, moderately priced childcare. This is essential in allowing parents to go out to work and often provides a positive learning environment for children. Any strategy which attempts to solve child poverty must address the issue of public childcare.

People with disabilities

Northern Ireland has a higher rate of disabled people than elsewhere in Britain. People who have a disability are much more likely to be in poverty and families, where someone has a disability, usually have a lower income. Disability – because of special needs – often has associated higher costs and those with a disability are also more likely to be unemployed.

Every war has its casualties and the devastation that poverty leaves in its wake affects many people but especially children. War leaves people powerless, trapped and fighting for survival. The poverty war causes suffering, psychological damage, social deprivation, family breakdown, ill-health and even death. When its toll is taken, children are always high among its victims.

Poverty is a war against children

1. Children born to parents living in poverty have a higher rate of infant mortality than those born to comfortably off parents.

2. Children born into families living in poverty have less chance of succeeding in education, usually because of a lack of books, a lack of a place to study, a lack of pre-school education and less access to schools with a high achievement record.

3. Children born into poverty – because of the lack of safe places to play – are likely to have more childhood accidents.

4. Children born into poverty are more likely to be ill and have less access to proper healthcare.

5. Children born into poverty if they stay in the same social class are more likely to die prematurely.

6. Children born into poverty are less likely to eat healthily usually because they can't afford to do so.

7. Children born into poverty are more likely to grow up in poverty and hence their children are also more likely to live in poverty.

8. Children living in poverty have less opportunity to fully participate in society because of the costs associated with doing so.

9. Poverty makes the accident of birth vital to your life chances, opportunities and future in society.

Poverty can and must be solved

The problems that poverty causes impact through the whole of society. Many people blame poor people themselves for their situation. Incredibly, some people say the poor aren't willing to take control of their lives, they won't work and they are happy to sponge off society. The reality is quite different. Most are responsible people who are trying against the odds to regain control of their lives but because of their economic and employment circumstances, they are fighting an unfair battle. Most people want work. Most want to participate in a meaningful way in society. Contrary to popular belief, instead of 'living off the system' there is a huge non-takeup of entitlements.

Behind the myths and the real life struggles of people living in poverty lies the empowering reality that poverty can be solved. The causes of poverty are easily identified. The solutions are also. Everyone knows that those solutions will cost. But the cost of the problems is greater than the cost of the solution. Save the Children has launched a major campaign to fight child poverty. We are making key policy recommendations which would address the poverty crisis. If you would like to know more, contact us today. Join our campaign for a more just society. For further information and address details, see page 39.

© Save the Children

A third of UK children living in poverty

When asked to imagine those living on inadequate incomes, many people think of pensioners, for obvious reasons. Yet now there is a group who outnumber pensioners as living in poverty in the UK – children and young people.

The Government's latest figures show that, in 1991-92, 4.1 million children lived in poverty, compared with 3.2 million pensioners. This compares with 1.4 million children and 1.5 million pensioners living in poverty in 1979. The definition of poverty is based on households living on below half of the average income. It shows that 32 per cent, nearly a third, of all children in the UK are now living in poverty. This compares with less than one in ten in 1979.

© Young People Now
March, 1995

Life's a struggle but a happy struggle

Kit Wharton meets a family trying to make ends meet below the poverty line

Paul and Georgina Stokes are providing a good home for three children on a disposable income teetering on what the Child Poverty Action Group would class as the poverty line.

A 30-year old computer technician working at Woolwich College in south London has a 'take-home' income after tax of about £730 a month, or $182.50 a week. Mrs Stokes's child benefit for three children is about £30 a week.

After they have paid rent of £56 a week for their council flat on the Aylesbury estate in South-west London, they are left with a disposable income of about £156.50 a week. That puts them on the edge of the poverty line according to the Child Poverty Action Group's estimate.

But the Stokeses are far from the stereotypical media view of the 'poor'. The couple's flat is warm, if cramped, and their three children are clearly very well cared for. Martyn, nine, and Victoria, five, go to the nearby Michael Farraday School, while six-week-old Alexandra gurgles happily on the floor.

There is no denying that meeting costs each week is not easy. 'Almost all purchases apart from food have to be made on hire purchase,' Mr Stokes says.

After bills are paid, the couple say they are lucky if they have £20 or £30 a month for luxuries. Mr Stokes has a car, but it has been in his father's garage for three years because he cannot afford the running costs. He goes to work on a small motorbike.

Mrs Stokes's one night out each week is as a member of the local darts team. Their last holiday was four years ago (a visit to Norfolk in a camper van) and the couple are waiting for a honeymoon, nine years after their marriage. Neither drinks nor smokes, and a luxury is a Chinese meal once in a while. The last time they went out to the cinema, Mrs Thatcher was in power.

Nor is the Aylesbury estate – where they live – the nicest place: a concrete jungle with much crime and one of the highest single-parent ratios in Britain.

Mr Stokes was mugged 20 feet from his front door five years ago by a man with a knife, who took his wallet and a gold chain with his mother's wedding ring on it. 'We hate living here but what can we do? We're stuck,' he says.

Both believe the rich are getting richer and the poor are getting poorer. 'Anyone who has got money in this country are getting more of it,' says Mr Stokes. 'Look at all these company chairmen. I would award myself a 75% pay rise if I could.' As it is Mr Stokes cannot even hope for overtime from his job because his employers cannot afford it.

Yet times are slightly easier now than they have been. Mr Stokes got his job last year after being unemployed for two years and taking a government retraining scheme.

Employment has made things easier, although the transition, when the couple lost benefits but were still waiting for wages to come through, was almost impossible.

Using catalogues and hire purchase, the family can afford a stereo system, colour television, fridge freezer, washing machine and microwave. The children are well clothed and have toys; and they have Pinky the cat.

What is also crucial is the extended family. Mr Stokes's father and Mrs Stokes's parents have helped out in the hard times with money or a bag of groceries.

'There are a lot of people richer than us,' Mr Stokes says. 'But there are people poorer than us too.'

© The Sunday Telegraph
February, 1995

The state of world poverty

After almost half a century of development aid, there are more poor people in the world, not less. The World Bank estimates that, in 1990, 1.1 billion people in Asia, Africa and Latin America were living on less than US $1 a day. That is a fifth of all humanity – and by 2000, they could number 1.3 billion.[1]

These are people who do not earn enough for an adequate diet, clothing, personal and household goods and shelter.[2]

The total number of poor rose in the last half of the 1980s, though the proportion declined overall. Only in East Asia and the Pacific did both the absolute numbers and the proportion of poor people drop in that period. In Latin America and the Caribbean, North Africa, and the Middle East and in Sub-Saharan Africa, both the number and proportion of poor people rose. In South Asia, the absolute numbers rose by 30 million people, but the proportion living in poverty fell by 2.8 per cent.

Estimates about the depth of poverty – that is, how far below the poverty line some people exist – reveal that in some regions the poor have also become poorer.

The 1980s were characterised by slow or negative economic growth and a drop in average incomes by as much as ten per cent in Latin America and more in sub-Saharan Africa. The crisis of the 1980s in Latin America, unleashed by the debt crisis and the economic squeeze that followed, affected both the middle-income and poorest groups. In countries such as Chile and Argentina, the number of households with incomes below the minimum needed to meet their basic needs doubled in the space of a few years.

Rising debt, and structural adjustment programmes (SAPs) set by the World Bank and the International Monetary Fund (IMF), also took their toll in Africa. The SAPs were in line with the free-market views of Western governments, and were imposed on cash-strapped countries.

While a previous over-emphasis on state intervention and planning made some adjustment inevitable, the social costs of SAPs fell on the poorest and most vulnerable people. The elimination of food subsidies may have helped farmers but it has hit the urban poor. Devaluation of domestic currencies, expected to favour exports, caused inflation and made imported food dearer.

Privatisation and a shrinking of the public sector cost large numbers of state employees their jobs. Cuts in spending on education, health and other social services hit the poor.[3]

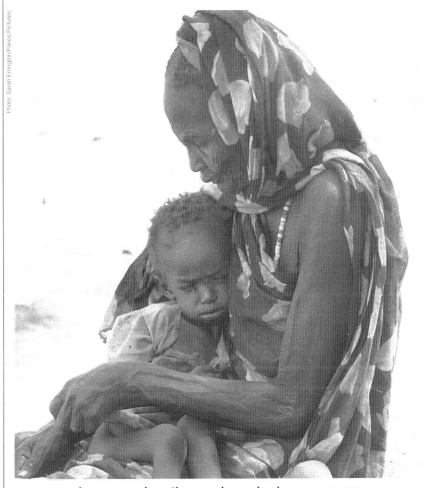

Photo: Sarah Errington/Panos Pictures

In some regions the poor have also become poorer

In the few countries where economic growth has resumed following structural adjustment, as in Chile, the numbers of the poor have declined much more slowly than they had risen during the recession.[4] Clearly there is more to poverty eradication than economic growth.

Defining poverty

The way poverty is measured is important because it determines objectives, and influences the poverty alleviation policies of governments and aid agencies. The complexities of poverty cannot be captured by drawing a line according to income. More complex indicators such as the Physical Quality of Life Index and the Human Development Index also measure the lack of safe drinking water and sanitation, primary health care and literacy. Two families may have similar incomes, but one will be better off than the other if it has access to free medicine and schooling, to running water and sanitation.

The Independent South Asian Commission on Poverty Alleviation has proposed that purchasing power measurements of poverty be supplemented by:
- Physical well-being, indicated by various scientific measures of mal-nutrition, especially of children;
- Quality of living environment, reflected by the quality of housing, access to safer water and sanitation.[5]

But as the Commission points out, poverty is not just a question of quantifiable indicators. It is also a question of vulnerability. A poor family is vulnerable if it lives in a flood-prone or landslide-prone area, or has no assets to sell if drought strikes. An older woman is vulnerable if she has nobody to support her.

The first priority of the poor is survival, followed closely by the desire for minimum security afforded by physical assets such as land and cattle. Other more intangible factors such as self-respect – being able to fend for oneself and to exercise some degree of choice – also become important once basic needs have been secured.

Sources

[1] *Implementing the World Bank's Strategy to Reduce Poverty – Progress and Challenges*, World Bank, April 1993.
[2] The World Bank definition of poverty according to levels of income is the one used for international comparisons, though it excludes other important factors such as land and cattle ownership and access to public services.
[3] *Survey of Economic and Social Conditions in Africa*, 1989-1990, United Nations, New York, 1992.
[4] *Latin American Poverty Profiles for the early 1990s*, ECLAC, Santiago, 1992, page 4.
[5] *Meeting the Challenge*, Report of the Independent South Asian Commission on Poverty Alleviation, SAARC, Kathmandu, November 1992.

The above is an extract from *The great aid robbery – How British aid fails the poor* available from the World Development Movement, see page 39 for address details

Poverty summit promises little

From *Christian Aid News*

Nowhere has the gap between rich and poor been more evident than at the United Nations poverty summit in Copenhagen in March. Some delegates from poorer countries could barely afford a cup of coffee in the conference centre, yet two of the richest countries hired lavish castles to accommodate their delegations, one reportedly costing $55,000 a night.

Like previous UN summits, Copenhagen has succeeded in forcing to the forefront issues which politicians too often leave on the back-burner. About 120 heads of state attended, putting poverty well and truly on the map. But like the Earth Summit in Brazil three years ago, the conference has largely let richer countries off the hook.

When the conference began, a number of imaginative ideas were under discussion. They included a proposal supported by Christian Aid to impose a 0.5 per cent tax on international currency speculation, which would have yielded enough money to triple aid spending.

In the end, however, the rich countries pledged next to nothing in terms of new resources to help the poor. Their complacency and cynicism ensured that the summit's final Declaration and Programme of Action were watered down. Some of the good ideas have survived, but there are no binding agreements to turn the rhetoric into reality.

Britain's lack of commitment to the summit was shown by the absence of the Prime Minister. British diplomats told a preparatory meeting last year that there was no need for Britain to be involved 'because there are no social problems in Britain'.

Words are the only tools Copenhagen has given the world's poor to fight injustice, but words can be powerful weapons. It is to be hoped that the spirit of the summit Declaration can be used to change hearts and minds and most importantly of all – government policies.

World faces 'health catastrophe'

By Liz Hunt
Medical Correspondent

Life expectancy in the world's poorest countries is likely to fall by 2000, according to the first global health survey. The report, by the World Health Organisation, points to poverty as the world's biggest killer, especially of children.

WHO says that one-fifth of the 5.6 billion people in the world live in extreme poverty; that almost one-third of the world's children are under-nourished, and that half the global population does not have access to essential drugs.

In 1993, more than 12 million children under the age of five died in the developing world – a figure which could have been cut to 350,000 if they had access to the same health care and nutrition as in wealthy countries. Chest infections in children, particularly pneumonia, kill at a rate of one child every eight seconds – 4 million annually and yet it costs less than 20 cents to treat, the report says.

Dr Hiroshi Nakijima, director-general of WHO, warns of a 'health catastrophe in which many of the great achievements . . .in recent decades will be thrown into reverse'.

Poverty-linked diseases such as cholera, tuberculosis and plague are on the rise in rich and poor countries alike, while rates of immunisation against fatal childhood diseases are dropping.

The report points to the 'neglected underclass' appearing in every city in the world: the elderly, the unemployed, the homeless, the street children and millions of women 'whose greatest disadvantage is their gender'. It also highlights the growing burden of the elderly as 'one of the most profound forces affecting health and social services in the next century'.

Population growth between 1990 and 2000 is estimated to be 17 per cent; the elderly will increase by 30 per cent. WHO predicts that care of elderly dementia patients and replacement of joints will be two of the most pressing demands on health care systems in the next century.

Globally, life expectancy at birth has increased to about 65 years but the difference between countries is a stark reminder of the growing inequity in health status, which means some countries spend less than $4 (£2.50) per person on health-care annually, WHO says.

In Japan, Sweden, and Iceland, life expectancy is 78 years or more. In the poorest countries the figure is 43 years and falling. By 2000, life expectancy in the Ivory Coast, the Central African Republic, Congo, Uganda and Zambia will have dropped to 42 years.

Infant mortality, one of the key indicators of a country's health, has fallen globally by 25 per cent, from 82 per 1,000 live births in 1980 to about 62. However, up to 320 out of 1,000 babies fail to reach their fifth birthdays in the poorest countries, compared with only 6 in the richest countries.

Maternal well-being varies dramatically – a pregnant woman in Africa is 13.5 times as likely to die in childbirth as her counterpart in Europe. More than 500,000 women die during labour or after delivery each year. Unsafe abortions account for 70,000 deaths.

● *The World Health Report 1995, Bridging the Gaps*, is published by the World Health Organisation, 1211 Geneva 27, Switzerland: Sfrl5.

© The Independent
May, 1995

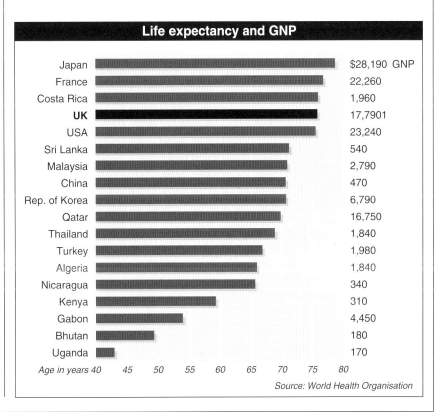

Life expectancy and GNP

Country		GNP
Japan		$28,190 GNP
France		22,260
Costa Rica		1,960
UK		17,7901
USA		23,240
Sri Lanka		540
Malaysia		2,790
China		470
Rep. of Korea		6,790
Qatar		16,750
Thailand		1,840
Turkey		1,980
Algeria		1,840
Nicaragua		340
Kenya		310
Gabon		4,450
Bhutan		180
Uganda		170

Age in years 40 45 50 55 60 65 70 75 80

Source: World Health Organisation

Famine myths – setting the record straight

This short briefing paper places some of the common myths about African famine in context. It updates the *Famine myths* published by Save the Children in 1991

Famine seems horribly familiar. It conjures up images of mass starvation and inevitability. But behind the numbing television images and statistics, are the facts that well known? Do those very images obscure reality, reducing people with a complex story to silent objects of pity?

News of famine often prompts such responses as 'they don't do enough to help themselves', 'they have too many babies' or 'there wouldn't be a famine if these countries spent less on arms'. We have all heard claims like these. But just how valid are they?

Famine in Africa often results from a lethal combination of factors – civil war, successive droughts and economic collapse. Many people are at the mercy of environmental, economic and political factors which are beyond their control. It is important to understand these. But, seen in isolation, they can obscure the true context of famine and fail to convey the tremendous efforts of local people to prevent famine happening – and how they cope when it does.

Myth 1

Famine is caused by over-population

Over-population is not a root cause of famine. Much of Africa is, in fact, very sparsely populated. Sub-Saharan Africa has an average population density of 16 people to every square kilometre. This compares with 258.3 people in the same area in India, 234.2 in the UK and 402.7 crowded into a square kilometre in Holland. Table 1 puts population density in context.

The whole continent has 20% of the world's cultivable land but only 9% of its people. Sub-Saharan Africa has fewer than 60 people per 100 hectares of cultivable land compared with an average ratio of 180 per 100 hectares for all developing countries. In fact, it has been suggested that there are not enough people to cultivate the land available.

There is evidence of a trend towards women having fewer children in Botswana, Zimbabwe, Kenya, Ghana, Sudan and Togo (*World Development Report 1992*, World Bank). On a global scale, population levels are a problem in some areas but the global relationship between famine and over-population is slight. For example, both China and India are far more densely populated than Africa, yet both have overcome famine.

Rapid population growth does not automatically put pressure on food resources. In many cases it has brought increased prosperity; examples include 19th century America,

Table 1	Population density
	Persons per sq. km
India	258.3
China	118.5
Malawi	72.0
Ethiopia	41.8
Liberia	23.4
Mozambique	19.5
Somalia	12.2
Sudan	8.2
Angola	8.0
UK	234.2
Holland	402.7

Source: *World Development Report 1992*, World Bank

and Hong Kong, Singapore and India. But population becomes a critical issue when there is a mismatch between the rate of population growth and the development of complementary resources such as irrigation, transport and health services. In some African countries, populations are expanding in an economic, political and environmental context that inhibits the growth of resources. To create the conditions necessary for bringing down birth rates, spending on health, education and social welfare must be increased – the very thing which the debt crisis prevents these countries from doing (see Myth 4).

It is simplistic to suggest that family planning can be imposed as a remedy for the problems facing impoverished Africans, and Save the Children does not advocate family planning by coercion. Large families do not lead to poverty. On the contrary, poverty leads to large families: poor parents have more children to shore up the security of the household, to provide labour on the land and carers for their old age.

People living in poorer countries where population growth rates are highest, consume a far smaller proportion of the earth's resources than people in richer countries. It is estimated that a child born in the USA will consume 25 times more resources than a child born in India.

Myth 2

Famine could be solved if governments spent less on the military

During the Cold War, many countries in Africa were the stage for superpower rivalries which directly fuelled instability across the continent. Though the Cold War has ended, its old victims suffer the aftermath in the Horn and Southern Africa. Western arms dealers and governments made huge profits from the sales of arms and other technical hardware to countries such as Somalia, which are now reaping the whirlwind of this era. 'During the 1980s,' writes journalist Jeremy Harding, 'Washington had provided at least $400 million in military aid to [former Somali president] Siad Barre' (*Small Wars, Small Mercies*, Viking, 1993).

The tables (below) set military spending in famine-hit Africa in context. Table 2 shows that there is no great difference between the proportion of national resources spent on the military by industrial and developing countries. But the least developed countries spend less than the industrial states, and Sub-Saharan Africa comes bottom of the league.

Table 3 shows how some of the countries recently hit by famine compare with other countries on military spending. In comparison with Nicaragua and Middle Eastern states facing similar regional insecurity, the proportion of GDP spent on arms is generally far lower in these countries. Civil wars in both Ethiopia and Mozambique have ended since these figures were released, so post-war spending is likely to be very different as these governments strive to rebuild their economies. For example, boosting the agricultural sector is a post-war priority in Ethiopia.

When defence spending is expressed as a percentage of total expenditure, the big spenders are United Arab Emirates (43.9%), Oman (41.1) and Syria (40.7). Zimbabwe, Liberia and Malawi trail behind at 16.5%, 9.8% and 5.4%, respectively. The USA and UK register 22.6% and 12.2% respectively (*World Development Report 1992*, World Bank).

However, between 1960 and 1989, the least developed countries nearly doubled the percentage of their GDP spent on the military. And some spend more today on this than on social services such as health

People living in poorer countries where population growth rates are highest, consume a far smaller proportion of the earth's resources than people in richer countries

and education. But it is misleading to suggest that governments choose to fight wars. The Cold War has left many countries with a legacy of armed banditry; cuts in the armed forces may not be a viable option for their governments.

Civil strife undoubtedly has a direct bearing on food crises. In a war zone, farmers cannot plant and tend crops and pastoralists find it difficult or impossible to feed, tend and trade their stock. Markets may close. Families are forced to leave home and give up trying to be self-sufficient. Thousands of displaced people flock to towns, putting great pressure on basic services and food

stocks. But war is not the sole cause of famine. In 1992, several drought-affected areas of Southern Africa – such as Zimbabwe – were free of conflict, as were parts of Sudan.

When war ends

Ironically, the end of war often exacerbates food crises.

- After the 1991 overthrow of the Ethiopian dictator Mengistu, some 400,000 Ethiopians who had fled to neighbouring countries returned home; many more have followed.
- Peace in Mozambique – the poorest country in the world – has brought the headache of

Table 2	Military expenditure
As % of gross domestic product (GDP)	
3.2%	Sub-Saharan Afric
4.1%	Least developed countries
4.4%	All developing countries
4.9%	Industrial countries
4.8%	World

Source: *Human Development Report 1992*, UNDP

Table 3	Military expenditure
As % of GDP, by country	
Rank order	%
Nicaragua	28.3
Iraq	23.0
Angola	21.5
Saudi Arabia	19.8
Oman	15.8
Ethiopia	13.6
Jordan	11.0
Mozambique	10.4
Israel	9.2
Zimbabwe	7.9
USA	5.8
Somalia	3.0
Liberia	2.2
Malawi	1.6

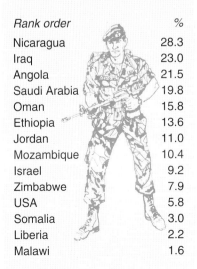

Source: *Human Development Report 1992*, UNDP

repatriating, resettling and feeding 1.5 million refugees, on top of the estimated four million people displaced in-country. The UN and agencies such as Save the Children are assisting in this process.

Myth 3

There is no point giving any money because nothing is ever done to deal with the root causes

Much is being done to tackle the root causes of famine but this long-term development work, unlike pictures of starving children, rarely makes the TV news headlines. Save the Children devotes around two-thirds of its annual overseas expenditure to development projects designed to make lasting improvements to the lives of children and families.

Examples of this type of development work include income generation schemes to boost family cashflow and improve nutrition (e.g. through a goat loan scheme in Sudan); revolving loan and credit schemes for villagers to see them through the hard times (e.g. in rural Mali); terracing schemes which prevent soil erosion (e.g. in Ethiopia); water conservation and tree-planting schemes which assist rainfed agri-culture (e.g. in North Darfur, Sudan); veterinary support for pastoralists (e.g. in Sudan and the Ogaden region); the supply of seeds, tools and fishing equipment to families that have lost their livelihoods to drought and famine (e.g. in Southern Sudan). Many Save the Children projects also focus on health care, enabling communities and governments to develop affordable and appropriate services and train local health workers.

The governments of famine-hit countries are also working to develop greater self-sufficiency, particularly in agriculture. These improvements are being achieved against all the odds. Few famine-hit countries have the capacity to fund investment in agriculture through their export earnings. The cards are stacked heavily against sustainable development. Many of the poorest African countries have to use a large proportion of their export earnings to service debt payments to the West (see Table 4), which far outstrip what they receive in aid.

Unfair terms of trade add to their financial problems: maize and sorghum, the principal grain products of Sudan and Ethiopia, have to compete with highly subsidised EC and US grain and import restrictions in the West. World prices for cash crops such as coffee have crashed, leaving producer countries unable to raise the foreign exchange necessary to pay for imports. Countless small farmers are also left struggling to cover the costs of growing and harvesting their crops in countries like Uganda, where 99.2% of export revenue once came from coffee. The import price of coffee on the London market fell from £4,175 per metric ton in 1977 to under £500 per ton in 1991 (*Africa South of the Sahara 1993*, Europa).

Processing industries in Africa are also up against it, hampered by tariff escalation – the practice by developed countries of charging higher tariffs on imports processed abroad (e.g. chocolate and cigarettes) than on the equivalent raw material (e.g. cocoa and tobacco). This protects Western processing industries and prevents poorer countries exporting manufactured goods.

Myth 4

People facing famine seem to do nothing to help themselves

Anyone who has watched a highland farmer in, say, Ethiopia, driving oxen and a rusty plough through heavy, parched soil at a gravity-defying angle, knows this statement is untrue. Rural people work round the clock to provide enough food for their families, the women of sub-Saharan Africa doing 50-80% of all agricultural labouring on top of running a home, caring for children, going to market, fetching water and so on. Only when all else fails are parents forced to sell their assets and leave their land and homes to search for food, work or aid.

When famine looms, people walk for miles to scavenge for wild foods like roots and berries. In Sudan, spring 1993 found whole communities reportedly subsisting on lilies and wild honey in the Nile swamplands (*The Observer*, 4 April

Table 4	The debt trap		
Country	Total long-term debt	Long-term debt as a ratio to GDP	Total long-term debt service
	(Millions US$)	%	%
Angola	7,217	64.9	36.4
Ethiopia	3,180	51.5	70.2
Malawi	1,609	73.9	18.0
Mozambique	4,739	363.3	93.2
Sudan	9,567	113.2	95.7
Uganda	1.787	38.5	73.9
Zimbabwe	2,684	42.0	30.2

Table 5	The trade trap	
Country	% change in export prices	% change in import prices
Ethiopia	−24.8	+9.7
Malawi	+10.1	+19.7
Mozambique	+18.6	+39.4
Somalia	+1,525.9	+2,399.3
Sudan	−9.1	+11.3

Price changes in the main exports compared with import prices.

Source: *Trends in Developing Economies 1992*, World Bank
Note: Sudan figures are for 1991, Somalia 1990.

TV images of passive crowds in emergency feeding centres give an incomplete picture

1993). If the worst happens and people become reliant on emergency food and medical relief, it is local people who usually spearhead relief programmes – not white expatriates, though the Western media focuses most attention on its own nationals, thus distorting the aid picture.

For example, in autumn 1992, at the height of the emergency in Somalia, Save the Children employed 750 local staff to 27 expatriate. Mogadishu's hospitals and clinics are run by Somali doctors and nurses, many of whom have worked without pay for months. In four camps for Somali refugees in eastern Ethiopia, where Save the Children runs emergency feeding programmes and clinics, it employs around 80 Ethiopians and 800 Somalis who are themselves refugees, many of them highly skilled doctors and community health workers.

TV images of passive crowds in emergency feeding centres give an incomplete picture. They show what happens when all else has failed: people who were once self-sufficient congregate where they hope food and medicine will be available.

At government level, the ability of countries to combat famine cannot be separated from their overall economic position. Many African countries are caught in a debt and trade trap. Tables 4 and 5 show the extent of these. The ability of

countries in Africa to buy food on world markets – an important strategy for those that are drought-prone – has fallen during the last decade because of rising poverty and a lack of foreign exchange and credit. A relatively solvent country like Zimbabwe was able to cope with famine in 1992 mostly through its own resources: it bought in 700,000 tonnes of grain, using a so-called 'soft' loan, having sold off its grain stocks to meet the terms of structural adjustment. A poorer country would not have been given such a loan. There are analogies with the position of poor people in the UK, who have to prove their ability to repay before being given a loan from the state's Social Fund. Countries, like families, have to show that they are not so poor that they are incapable of repaying a loan.

Myth 5

We are always hearing about famine. Africa seems to face famines every year… they are inevitable

Famine is not something which happens year in, year out. While drought in sub-Saharan Africa is a fact of life, famine – in the sense of mass starvation – has been rare. And countries which experience droughts and crop failures can overcome food shortages, though this is done at great cost to the economy.

Famine-hit countries may have grown enough food to feed their people, but if this has been produced for export it is not available to those in need. It has to be sold to generate foreign exchange to pay off debts and the interest on loans, thereby satisfying the conditions of the big donors.

Famines are not inevitable, in Africa or elsewhere. A number of drought-prone countries have successfully developed the economic resources to survive difficult periods. India, for example, has set up a national food security system which has prevented major droughts from leading to famine – without the need to seek external aid. India now sends food aid to Africa.

Botswana and a number of other drought-prone African countries have managed to avoid famine by devising schemes to help the most vulnerable communities through periods of food shortage. They include free food distribution, supplementary feeding for school-children and cash-for-work projects. (For a fuller answer, see also Myths 3 and 4).

If disaster does strike, national infrastructure – e.g. road and rail transport – is crucial to the delivery, of relief. Large-scale food aid operations in countries with poor infrastructure are unavoidably slow. Infrastructure has been particularly affected by the debt crisis and International Monetary Fund (IMF) adjustment programmes.

The myths addressed in this briefing are often cited in debates about famine. They are frequently used as excuses for ignoring the plight faced by famine-hit communities. The reality, however, is much more complicated and closer to home – North and South are interdependent, and issues of debt, trade and food involve consumers in the UK as well as Africa. Myths operate at the level of half truths which ignore the wider interaction of economic, political and social factors.

• The above is an extract from *Famine Myths*. Copies of the leaflet are available from Save the Children. See page 39 for address details.

Simply... making the food go around

Environmental protection

Overpopulation in the Majority World has often been blamed for ecological catastrophe. In fact poor people have more at stake in preserving the resources they depend on. It is ruthless, short-sighted commercial exploitation by the rich which is levelling the Amazon forests for furniture, narcotics and beefsteak. Plantations grow the same crop repeatedly, earmarking their produce for the West. Such practices supply the whims of 'developed' nations, leaving all the costs in the South. To preserve a common future, the environment must take priority. We can help by encouraging green produce and questioning our own consumption.

Fair trade

The terms of international trade favour wealth absolutely. The rich world keeps the South wedded to commodity production by putting up tariff barriers to manufactured goods. Barriers to textiles and clothing alone cost poor countries $53 billion a year in lost trade – this equals the total of all Western aid to the South. Ironically, maintaining poverty in the Majority World means poor countries can buy fewer of the manufactured goods the rich are so eager to supply. There is no such thing as a 'free' market; what we have to strive for is one that is fair. The first step is to get informed and use our choices as consumers and investors wisely. As citizens we can oppose unfair trade and voice that opposition to our political leaders.

Appropriate agriculture

There is no quick fix for areas with food shortages – the answers for each region are specific to it. The Green Revolution got hijacked by rich élites who priced small farmers out of the market. In industrial countries commercial farming, propped up with

Global food surpluses and hunger don't add up. As long as the politics of greed continues to thrive, people will stay hungry. But is feeding the world just pie in the sky – or can it be for real?

subsidies, continues apace with its arsenal of polluting chemicals, its pesticide-resistant pests and declining yields. The real answers lie elsewhere, with the farmers who make the best use of their lands, fighting pests with pests, growing a variety of crops to keep the soil fertile, saving the best seeds for the future. For their efforts to succeed, they must be able to make their own decisions instead of having governments, big agribusiness companies and policy makers on the other side of the globe (such as the World Bank and the IMF) setting out chapter and verse.

Equal rights for women

Women inherit every disadvantage and none of the power. They work more hours than men – yet 70 per cent of the world's adult poor are women. Four hundred million women of childbearing age weigh less than 100 pounds – their malnutrition is passed on to their infants. In 'developed' countries women earn half as much as men. Often their work may not even be counted as work. Women produce half the world's food and own 1 per cent of its farmlands. Equality with men is the basic issue. The best way to attack women's hunger is by improving access to fairly paid work and to land. Education also improves women's control over their fertility, their health and standard of living.

Land reform

A billion people living in the villages of the Majority World have no land of their own to farm. Two-thirds of them live in India and Bangladesh. In Guatemala and Peru 85 per cent of rural workers are landless. Wherever the problem exists there

The real answers lie with the farmers who make the best use of their land

is usually a history of thwarted land-reform movements – thwarted by the bigwigs who own the land and have political clout. Giving land to poor farmers so they can grow their own food would not work on its own. It would have to be backed by improved access to credit and the means of production, like machinery. But land reform could create the jobs in the countryside which poor people from rural areas seek in city slums.

Peace

War causes hunger – whether in Iraq reeling under economic sanctions after the Gulf War or in Afghanistan where 15 years of fighting have wrecked food production. Conflict robs people of homes and livelihoods – refugees have no land to grow food and no work to enable them to buy it. The world spent $767 billion in 1994 on its military might – more than the total income of the poorest 45 per cent of the world's population. The 'peace dividend' has yielded $935 billion since 1987 through reduced arms spending, but none of it has gone towards international development aid. We need to lobby our leaders to work for peace and to use its dividends wisely. Greater stability would give poorer nations the opportunity to reduce their own military expenditure.

Sharing the wealth

More than a billion people live on less than a dollar a day. The wealthiest one-fifth of the world's people control about 85 per cent of the money, the poorest fifth about 1.4 per cent. Cant about the free market creating opportunities for poor people is meaningless when wealth calls all the shots. Filthy-rich individuals apart, the politics of greed makes no economic sense for the wealthy countries that pursue it. Economic success in the Majority World would mean increased trade and more, rather than fewer, jobs in the West. By sharing wealth, we could actually be safeguarding it.

Building community

Gross inequality is not just about economics; it is about moral choice. We need to replace the harmful myth of the individual making a killing – so important to modern imperialism – with the idea of the individual within a community. People aware of their connectedness can build both compassion and strength. Many poor communities with little to spare are working towards this ideal – whether it's poor women running communal soup kitchens in Peru and Bolivia, or farmers across Latin America involved in a programme to exchange knowledge. The real New World Order starts here.

© *New Internationalist*
May, 1995

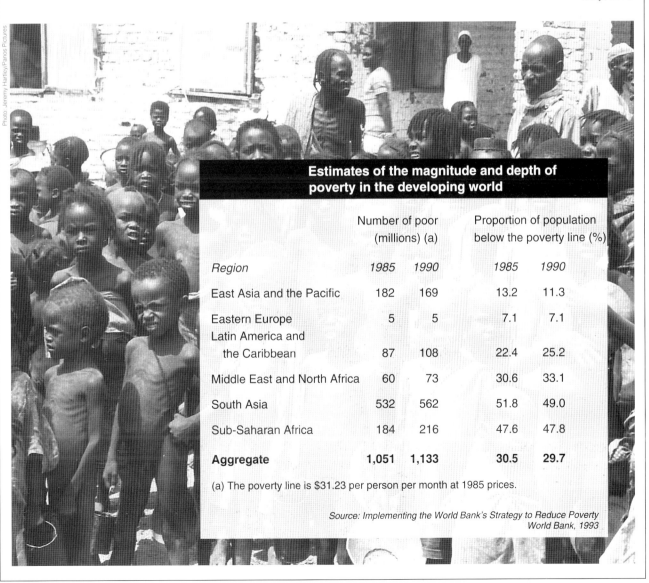

Estimates of the magnitude and depth of poverty in the developing world

Region	Number of poor (millions) (a)		Proportion of population below the poverty line (%)	
	1985	1990	1985	1990
East Asia and the Pacific	182	169	13.2	11.3
Eastern Europe	5	5	7.1	7.1
Latin America and the Caribbean	87	108	22.4	25.2
Middle East and North Africa	60	73	30.6	33.1
South Asia	532	562	51.8	49.0
Sub-Saharan Africa	184	216	47.6	47.8
Aggregate	**1,051**	**1,133**	**30.5**	**29.7**

(a) The poverty line is $31.23 per person per month at 1985 prices.

Source: *Implementing the World Bank's Strategy to Reduce Poverty*
World Bank, 1993

Hunger – the facts

The world produces more than enough food to feed its entire population. Yet an estimated 35,000 people die of hunger each day. The *New Internationalist* examines the gap between the hungry and the greedy

The scale of it[1]

The number of hungry people in the world has actually fallen in recent years, despite overall population increases. But nearly 800 million people still face persistent, everyday hunger. Much larger numbers suffer from malnutrition and seasonal or temporary hunger.

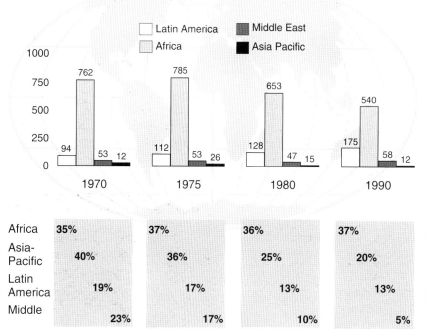

Number of undernourished people in millions

Legend: Latin America, Africa, Middle East, Asia Pacific

	1970	1975	1980	1990
Latin America	94	112	128	175
Africa	762	785	653	540
Middle East	53	53	47	58
Asia Pacific	12	26	15	12

	1970	1975	1980	1990
Africa	35%	37%	36%	37%
Asia-Pacific	40%	36%	25%	20%
Latin America	19%	17%	13%	13%
Middle	23%	17%	10%	5%

Percentage of population

Desert blooms[2]

The countries with the highest rates of agricultural growth are relatively rich nations making the desert bloom. Saudi Arabia has become the sixth-largest wheat exporter in the world.[3]

Highest agricultural growth 1980-91

Average annual % increase in real terms

1	Saudi Arabia	14.0
2	Jordan	8.1
3	Oman	7.1
4	Morocco	6.8

Eating money

Richer countries can choose; they have ample access to food and are less dependent on agriculture. The US is the world's second-largest producer of cereals and meat and comes third in fruit and vegetable production – yet agriculture accounts for only 2.3% of its GDP. European Union countries import twice as many agricultural products from the Majority World as they export to them.[3] Poorer countries have little or no choice.

Shares of the crop

The rich world's proportion of grain production is significantly higher than its share of the world population.

	% of world production[6]	% of world population[7]
Africa	5.5	12.4
North America (USA & Canada)	18.2	5.2
Central & South America	6.7	8.4
Asia	52.7	59.0
Europe	15.2	14.5
Oceania	1.7	0.5

Photo: Heidur Netocny/Panos Pictures

Craving for cash

Cash crops are the only things some countries can export. But such crops take up land which could be used for growing food for local consumption. This wouldn't matter if the terms of trade were fair and cash-crop prices were higher. Cocoa shows how poorer countries provide for a hunger for chocolate in the rich world.

COCOA

Top 10 producers

		'000 tonnes[2]	Income (GNP per capita in US$, 1992)[1]
1	Côte d'Ivoire	747	670
2	Brazil	290	2,770
3	Ghana	243	450
4	Malaysia	220	2,790
5	Indonesia	180	670
6	Nigeria	110	320
7	Cameroon	105	820
8	Ecuador	85	1,070
9	Colombia	50	1,290
10	Dominican Rep.	48	1,040

Top 10 consumers

		'000 tonnes[2]	Income (GNP per capita in US$, 1992)[1]
1	United States	593	23,120
2	Germany	264	23,030
3	United Kingdom	180	17,760
4	France	160	22,300
5	Japan	111	28,220
6	Brazil	73	2,770
7	Italy	73	20,510
8	Spain	60	14,020
9	Belgium	57	20,880
10	Canada	49	20,320

Of all the money spent on chocolate in Britain, 15% goes to the Treasury and only 8% to the cocoa farmer.[5]

Feast and famine[7]

The rich world has a glut – of food and obese citizens: in the US about a third of the population is overweight – $33 billion is spent each year in attempts to lose weight. In the poor world millions subsist on an amount of food that is simply inadequate for good health. An estimated 190 million children under the age of five are chronically malnourished.

THE FEAST
Countries with highest daily supply of calories per head as % of requirements* 1988-90

Ireland	157
Greece	151
Belgium	149
Bulgaria	148
France	143
Spain	141
Italy	139
US	138
Hungary	137
Singapore	136
Aotearoa/NZ	130
UK	130
South Africa	128
Australia	124

THE FAMINE
Countries with lowest daily supply of calories per head as % of requirements* 1988-90

72	Afghanistan
73	Chad
73	Ethiopia
77	Mozambique
80	Angola
81	Somalia
82	Central African Republic
82	Rwanda
83	Sierra Leone
84	Burundi
84	Bolivia

Shocking as they may be, these figures are only averages. There are hungry people in rich countries and those who can afford more than they need in poorer ones, which makes the contrast between greed and need even more dramatic.

*An adequate adult calorie intake is about 2,350 and 2,600 calories per day, depending on climate and kinds of work performed.

Grain for meat[3]

Farm animals consume nearly half the world's cereal produce. Growing grain to feed animals to turn them into meat is an inefficient business – an acre of cereals can produce five times more protein than an acre devoted to meat production.

World cereal use (1988-90)

HUMAN 822 million tonnes
ANIMAL 642 million tonnes

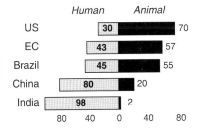

As a % of total cereal available, selected regions, 1990.

	Human	Animal
US	30	70
EC	43	57
Brazil	45	55
China	80	20
India	98	2

80 40 0 40 80

Sources

[1] Bread for the World Institute, *Hunger 1995; Causes of Hunger*, Silver Spring, 1994.
[2] The Economist, *Pocket World in Figures* 1995.
[3] Bertrand Delpeuch, *Seed and Surplus*, CIIR/ Farmers Link, London, 1994.
[4] The World Bank, *World Development Report 1993*.
[5] World Development Movement.
[6] FAO, *Production Yearbook 1993*.
[7] UNICEF, *The State of the World's Children 1995*.

© *New Internationalist* May, 1995

Rooting out poverty

From ACTIONAID

On current trends, the poverty reduction targets agreed by the international community for the year 2000 will not be met in:

Health

Goal set	One-third reduction in under-5 mortality
Forecast	More than half of the developing countries with high child mortality rates are unlikely to reach the target

Water

Goal set	Universal access to safe water
Forecast	770 million people will still be without safe water

Education

Goal set	Basic education for all children
Forecast	100 million children will still not be enrolled in primary school

The number of people living in absolute poverty is increasing by around 26 million a year. This trend suggests that the number of absolute poor will rise from the current 1.3 billion to over 1.5 billion by 2000.

The key measures needed to root out poverty are known. Universal access to basic health care, safe water and primary education are achievable goals. Great strides in improving the quality of life can be made by policy changes and a better use of resources.

The reality of increasing poverty . . .

An additional 26 million people equivalent to just under half the UK's population – are falling into the trap of absolute poverty every year. The number of absolute poor is growing in sub-Saharan Africa and Latin America, where the percentage of people living in absolute poverty is already 54 per cent and 28 per cent, respectively. Poverty is falling in Asia, though six out of every ten people in South Asia still live in absolute poverty[1].

In Africa, the number of absolute poor increased by almost 50 per cent between 1988 and 1990, from 200 million to nearly 300 million people. The numbers of rural poor in developing countries, who account for 80 per cent of the world's poor, are projected by the International Fund for Agricultural Development to grow to 1310 million by the year 2000[2]. Globally, the increase in the rate of population growth is comparable to the rise in the numbers of those living in absolute poverty.

Rising poverty

A recent World Bank study found that the percentage of the population living in poverty was rising in 14 out of 37 countries surveyed, contributing to a global increase of 2 per cent per year.

% in absolute poverty		
Country	*1985*	*1990*
China	11.1	13.5
Bolivia	10.7	17.8
Brazil	26.7	35.3
Dominican Rep.	24.2	24.3
Honduras	58.7	62.3
Jordan	4.2	12.6
Bangladesh	16.8	27.8
Mexico	22.1	22.6
Panama	25.1	27.5
Peru	15.2	31.0
Cote d'Ivoire	14.3	20.2
Ethiopia	58.7	69.1
Rwanda	56.2	76.4
Venezuela	7.3	20.6

Source: World Bank, Is Poverty Increasing in the Developing World? June 1993

. . .and of rooting out poverty

The fact that poverty can be reduced is witnessed in the progress made by developing countries in recent decades and in the daily experience of non-governmental development agencies such as ACTIONAID. Yet the rising number of people in poverty highlights the immense task which lies ahead. The world has sufficient resources and know-how to make a serious assault on poverty in the coming decades. What is required is the will to ensure that poverty reduction is prioritised. Significantly reducing the numbers of people who live in absolute poverty requires not only additional resources but also policy changes which take account of the complexity of the task and which seek to put the needs of poor people at the centre of policy-making. To work effectively with the poor requires a thorough understanding of the causes of poverty in each and every place, and especially an understanding of how people themselves perceive poverty – what it means for them. Too often, people assume that as outsiders they can define poverty; the solutions they then seek to develop become pre-packaged, and may fail. Poverty reduction work should be rooted in the perspectives of the poor and too limited an understanding of poverty can strip dignity and self-respect from those who have little else.

Progress is possible

Between 1950 and 1990 the number of children dying before their fifth birthday fell from 28 to 10 out of every hundred in developing countries.

Between 1960 and 1990 the proportion of children enrolled in primary school rose from 48 to 78 per cent in developing countries.

Between 1970 and 1990 life expectancy increased from 53 to 62 years in developing countries.

Photo: Adrian Arbib/ACTIONAID

The proportion of families with access to safe drinking water has risen

Since 1980, the proportion of families with access to safe drinking water has risen from 38 to 68 per cent in South East Asia, from 66 to 78 per cent in Latin America and from 32 to 43 per cent in Africa.

What is poverty?

Poverty is complex to define and involves considerations other than lack of material factors, such as income. Poverty also relates to self-perception, the perception of others and to a fundamental lack of opportunity and of choices and its nature will vary according to particular social or cultural circumstances. Attempts to quantify poverty can therefore be problematic but some quantification is required to gauge disparities within countries and to assess trends. For the statistics in this briefing, we have followed the standard definition of poverty used by the World Bank: per capita incomes of no more than $370 (£246) per year – equivalent to less than 66 pence a day. This figure, which the World Bank recognises to be somewhat arbitrary, takes account of the spending required to buy a minimum standard of basic necessities. We have also taken as a key reference point the experience of poverty of many of the communities with whom ACTIONAID works – lack of access to basic amenities such as health care, education and safe drinking water.

. . .and who are the poor?

While the situation varies from country to country, the poor tend to be:

- the landless or small land owners
- nomadic herders
- households headed by women
- hunters and gatherers
- low-wage urban workers or unemployed
- refugees and displaced people
- marginalised ethnic indigenous populations.

Sources

[1] World Bank, *Is Poverty Increasing in the Developing World?*, June 1993.
[2] IFAD, *The State of World Rural Poverty*, 1993.

© ACTIONAID
June, 1994

Poverty factors

Percentage of people without access to Health Services[*]

Sub-Saharan Africa	44
Middle East/North Africa	22
South Asia	48
East Asia/Pacific	13
Latin America/Caribbean	26

Percentage of males who are illiterate

Sub-Saharan Africa	39
Middle East/North Africa	30
South Asia	41
East Asia/Pacific	14
Latin America/Caribbean	13

Percentage of females who are illiterate

Sub-Saharan Africa	59
Middle East/North Africa	54
South Asia	20
East Asia/Pacific	33
Latin America/Caribbean	17

Percentage of people without access to safe water

Sub-Saharan Africa	57
Middle East/North Africa	23
South Asia	20
East Asia/Pacific	32
Latin America/Caribbean	22

* Lack of access to Health Services is defined as the percentage of the population who cannot reach appropriate local health services by the local means of transport in under an hour.

Source: UNICEF
State of the World's Children
1994

© ACTIONAID
June, 1994

Women and poverty

The Women's National Commission (WNC) feels strongly that there can be no genuine development for women whilst they form 62 per cent of the poor [*Poverty: The Facts*, Carey Oppenheim, Child Poverty Action Group, 1990] living in a society with enormous and increasing discrepancies in wealth. UK official statistics indicate that the incomes of the poor have deteriorated by 14 per cent over the last decade whilst average incomes of the wealthy have increased by 36 per cent (*DSS Households Below Average Income* HMSO, 1993.

Poverty can mean the denial of basic opportunities to participate in civic and social life and also to education and self-improvement, with a consequent denial of opportunities to improve one's earnings and circumstances. The poverty of women is directly related to the status and reward attached to traditional women's roles. Measures to remove the causes of poverty must address the fundamental position of women in the economy.

The predominant cause of women's poverty is the dichotomy between family responsibilities and external employment. Whilst the requirement for women to contribute to the family upkeep or support themselves has steadily increased in recent years, the pattern of working life has been slow to adapt to families' domestic commitments. It is overwhelmingly women who remain responsible for the upbringing of children and the care of elderly and infirm relatives. With these responsibilities their opportunities for paid employment, regardless of education, have been strictly curtailed. Jobs which are designated as 'suitable' for women are characterised by requiring (and receiving) little training, offering no hope of promotion and none of the rights of the full time employee, e.g. child minders, care assistants. Women accept these posts because they need to work within easy travelling distance of home. They have no power to bargain with employers for better conditions, and can be neglected by trade unions.

The poverty of women is directly related to the status and reward attached to traditional women's roles

---

Poverty and dependency

In 1990/91 a study [Esam, P and Berthoud, R (1991) *Independent Benefits for Men and Women* (London: Policy Studies Institute)] estimated that 4.6 million women, compared with 0.4 million men, had independent incomes of less than £25 per week. Women are ten times more likely than men to have very low incomes. The low independent incomes of women makes them dependent on others to avoid poverty whether that dependence is on state benefits or on another wage in the family.

60 per cent of adults for whom income support is paid are women; 32 per cent of widows and 70 per cent of lone mothers are dependent on income support. [Glendinning, C and Millar, J eds, *Women and Poverty in Britain in the 1990s* (London: Harvester Wheatsheaf)] Women are more likely than men to have little or no income and few assets. The limited financial independence of women as a group also limits their capacity to accumulate wealth and assets. Women on their own with children are the group most likely to be dependent on welfare benefits.

The priority must be to raise the income earning potential of women and provide support for women to provide an independent income for themselves.

● The above is an extract from *In Search of Equality, Development and Peace*.

© *Women's National Commission*

Poor nations shame rich in UNICEF rankings

Britain and many of the industrialised countries are not doing as much for their citizens as parts of the Third World. A United Nations report measuring political participation and provision of health care, education and other needs against GNP shows many nations wielding economic and military power falling short

Rich nations, usually judged by their economic and military strength, fall far short of many of the weakest and poorest countries of the world in the human measures which really count in measuring the richness of civilisation.

The United Nations Children's Fund's latest *Progress of Nations* report throws up surprising stars – such as Bangladesh, China, Cuba and Albania – when it comes to standards of health, education, access to clean water, political participation and care for the vulnerable and disadvantaged. Their records con-trast with shaming figures for Saudi Arabia, Turkey and Indonesia in under-five mortality, though in the latter two countries a child who does survive has a fair chance of education.

The UN report ranks countries' performance against the level which would be expected from their gross national product.

The Progress of Nations also records the darker side of societies rich and poor in their treatment of women and girls. Sexual exploitation of children is one of the gravest infringements of human rights, UNICEF says.

'Like child labour it is every-where . . .it runs the sordid gamut from incest and sexual abuse by friends and family members to the enforced, servile marriage of the too-young girl, to the systematic commercial plundering of children and young teenagers in lucrative prostitution and pornography markets.'

The United States, for instance, has 300,000 people under 18 in-volved in prostitution.

By Victoria Brittain

Britain comes under fire for lagging well behind some of the poorest countries in the percentage of women in parliament. The British score for female Members of Parliament of 9 per cent is only half the average for industrialised countries, and compares with 16 and 17 per cent in countries like Rwanda, Uganda, Mozambique, Argentina and Nicaragua.

UNICEF's league table ranking countries according to the proportion of women in parliament places Sweden at the top with 42 per cent. Other Scandinavian countries score over 30 per cent, while South Africa, Cuba, China and North Korea are over 20 per cent.

Among industrialised countries only Australia, France, Greece and Japan, with scores of 8, 6, 6 and 3 per cent, show up worse than Britain. The United States is slightly better, but despite much hype about recent gains for women, still has only 11 per cent.

Britain's 9 per cent is the average figure for the world and, in a surprising finding, UNICEF indicates that there has actually been a decline in the world average which was 15 per cent in 1988.

There are still countries – including Bahrain, Kuwait and the United Arab Emirates – where women can neither stand for election nor vote. Overall for the Middle East, the worst region of the world on most of the indicators, the average is 3 per cent.

These UNICEF tables highlight the credibility problem facing the United Nations conference on women, due to open in Beijing in September. After a UN decade for women, and three major UN con-ferences, progress towards equality in this key area has been poor.

UNICEF also reveals the poor performance of Britain in another area directly related to women's rights, the increasingly female face of poverty, and to the hopes of the Beijing conference: overseas aid. Twenty-five years ago the UN committed itself to aid at the level of 0.7 per cent of each donor country's gross national product. Britain is one of several countries moving away from the target, with a score of 0.31 per cent in 1992 and 0.28 per cent in 1993. The United States is in bottom place with a contribution of 0.15 per cent of GNP. Again the four Scandinavian countries come top of the league, all meeting the UN target.

The implications of these trends for world security are grave. Richard Jolly, deputy executive director of UNICEF, warns that 'the industri-alised nations that still control three-quarters of the world's wealth and dominate the structures of trade, aid and finance' have not taken seriously the challenge of changing world economic policies and priorities.

Progress in the human condi-tion, he points out in the report, will never come about as a result of solely economic advance. The fundamental problem is 'achieving sustainable economic growth and ensuring its more equitable distribution'.

© *The Guardian*
June, 1995

Child neglect in rich nations

Poverty amid plenty

Life is becoming harder for children in some key industrialized countries. Slowly but surely over the last 15 years, some of the world's most powerful economies have tilted in an ominous new direction – towards the devaluation of children – flouting the conventional wisdom that child neglect and deprivation have no place in rich nations. Most dramatically in the United States, but also in Australia, Canada, New Zealand and the United Kingdom, a significant number of children are failing to thrive.

The United States has by far the highest percentage of children living in poverty: 20 per cent, which represents a 21 per cent increase since 1970. Three other 'Anglo-American' countries – Australia, Canada and the United Kingdom – are at or near the 9 per cent mark. Yet, in most other rich countries, child poverty rates are a fraction of the United States rate.[1] In Western Europe and Japan, for example, child poverty rates typically hover around 2 to 5 per cent.[2]

The problems of children in Anglo-American nations today range from elemental issues of safety and shelter to more complicated issues of psychic health and educational performance. Child poverty rates, school drop-out rates and teenage suicide rates are all on the rise. In the United States, Scholastic Aptitude Test (SAT) scores for college-bound students are 70 points lower than they were 20 years ago. In the United Kingdom, the number of adolescents taking their own lives grew by 41 per cent during the 1980s. In New Zealand, the number of reported child-abuse cases has doubled in six years. And in Australia, the number of homeless children has increased by a third since 1980. According to one recent blue ribbon committee, 'Never before has one generation of children been less

healthy, less cared for or less prepared for life than their parents were at the same age.'[3]

These tendencies are particularly ironic given the new level of public commitment to children by world leaders. At the World Summit for Children, held in September 1990 at United Nations Headquarters in New York and attended by approximately half the world's Presidents and Prime Ministers, governments formally adopted a set of goals to improve the life circumstances of children. These included controlling major childhood diseases, halving the incidence of child malnutrition and reducing by a third the death rate in children under five years old. Most countries agreed to draw up national programmes of action to implement the goals.

Despite such impressive initiatives, a large gap between rhetoric and reality remains. A case in point: The 1990 World Summit urged all countries to ratify the Convention on the Rights of the Child, a document seeking to lay down minimum standards for the survival, protection and development of all children. As of 31 August 1993, 146 nations had ratified it; the United States has yet to do so. But without

the full commitment to young people of the world's richest democracy, we cannot go beyond 'the edge of a new era of concern for the silent and invisible tragedy that poverty inflicts on today's children and on tomorrow's world.'[4]

The root causes of child neglect in rich nations have to do with new forms of scarcity in both public resources and parental time. In the financial sphere, policy-makers display a weak and eroding commitment to children. For example, during the 1980s, governments pursuing *laissez faire* policies reduced housing budgets, cut back on welfare payments to poor families and denied large numbers of working mothers the right to spend a few weeks at home with their newborn babies.

In the United States during that decade, less than 5 per cent of the federal budget was spent on programmes that supported families with children, while approximately 24 per cent of federal resources was spent on persons over the age of 65.[5] Canada followed a similar pattern. By 1990, per capita government spending on senior citizens was 2.7 times greater than that allocated to the young.[6] In these two countries, at least, the resources invested at the beginning of life are now dwarfed by the resources consumed at the end of life. American and Canadian policy makers have tended to socialise the costs of growing old and to privatise childhood at a time when fragile family structures make it particularly difficult for parents to carry the entire child-raising load.

In the Anglo-American world, this failure to invest public money in children has been aggravated by a growing time deficit. Over the last two decades there has been a sharp decline in the amount of time parents spend caring for their children, a trend that has been particularly pronounced in the United Kingdom and the United States. According to Stanford University economist Victor Fuchs, American children have lost 10 to 12 hours of parental time per week.[7] The time parents have available for their children has been squeezed by the rapid shift of mothers into the paid labour force, by escalating divorce rates and the abandonment of children by their fathers, and by an increase in the number of hours required on the job. In the United States, the average worker is now at work 163 hours a year more than in 1967, which adds up to an extra month of work annually.[8] In a similar vein, time spent on the job in the United Kingdom increased by two hours a week during the 1980s.

Much of this new parental time pressure is, of course, involuntary, provoked by falling wage rates and escalating housing costs. But whatever the reasons behind the parental time deficit, it has had extremely negative effects on children. Unsupervised 'latchkey' children are at increased risk of substance abuse, and children with little or no contact with their fathers are less likely to perform well at school.

The failure to invest either public resources or private time in the raising of children has left millions of youngsters in this important group of Anglo-American cultures fending for themselves, and coping more or less badly with the difficult business of growing up in the 1990s. True, many children continue to be raised in supportive communities by thoughtful, attentive parents; but looming larger is the overall drift, in both government policy and private adult choices, towards blighting youngsters and stunting their potential. An anti-child spirit is loose in these lands.

In contrast, the negative trends have not extended to continental Europe – or to Japan, for that matter. In the traditionally Catholic countries of southern Europe, families and communities have remained strong enough to continue to provide a supportive environment for raising children, despite some slippage over the last decade. And in the welfare states of Scandinavia, comprehensive and aggressive social policies have compensated for family disintegration and created conditions that allow children to flourish. What these nations share is a wider and deeper vision of collective responsibility for children.

● The above is an extract from the booklet *Child neglect in rich nations* available from UNICEF (UK), see page 39 for address details.

Sources

[1] Smeeding, Timothy M., 'The War on Poverty: What Worked?, 25 September 1991, testimony prepared for the Joint Economic Committee, US Congress. See also: John Code, Lee Rainwater and Timothy Smeeding, *American Economic Association Papers and Proceedings*, 'Inequality Among Children and Elderly in Ten Modern Nations: The United States in an International Context', American Economic Association, Nashville, Tenn., May 1989, p. 323.

[2] Innnocenti Occasional Papers, UNICEF, International Child Development Centre, Florence, 1990. Cornia, Giovanni Andrea, 'Child Poverty and Deprivation in Industrialized Countries: Recent Trends and Policy Options' (No. 2, p. 29). Jonathan Bradshaw, 'Child Poverty and Deprivation in the UK' (No. 8, p. 8). Using a different measure, Bradshaw shows a startling rise in child poverty in the UK; in his study the child poverty rate rises from 9 per cent in 1980 to 18 per cent in 1985.

[3] National Commission on the Role of the School and the Community in Improving Adolescent Health, *Code Blue: Uniting for Healthier Youth*, National Association of State Boards of Education and the American Medical Association, Washington DC, 1990, p. 3.

[4] United Nations Children's Fund (UNICEF), *The State of the World's Children 1993*, Oxford University Press, 1992, p. 58.

[5] Smeeding, Timothy M., 'The Debt, the Deficit and the Disadvantaged Children: Generational Impacts and Age, Period and Cohort Effects', in *The Debt and the Twin Deficits Debate*, ed. James M. Rock, Bristlecone Books/Mayfield, Mountain View, California, 1991, p. 47.

[6] Ng, Edward, 'Children and Elderly People: Sharing Public Income Resources', Canadian Social Trends, Statistics Canada, Summer 1992, p. 15.

[7] Fuchs, Victor R., *Women's Quest for Economic Equality*, Harvard University Press, Cambridge, Mass., 1988, p. 111.

[8] Schor, Juilet B., *The Overworked American: The Unexpected Decline of Leisure*, Basic Books, New York, 1992, p. 28.

[9] Hewitt, Patricia, *About Time: The Revolution in Work and Family Life*, IPPR Rivers Oram Press, London, 1993, p. 16. These figures refer to average male manual workers' hours.

© UNICEF

Child poverty in rich nations: Where taxes and transfers help the least

The UK and the US have the highest child poverty rates among the eight industrialised countries shown below – 27.9% and 22.3% respectively of their children 17 years or younger live below 40% of the adjusted median family income, according to 1986 figures. France also has a high child poverty rate – 21.2%, according to 1984 data. However, while France and the other continental European countries reduce their child poverty rates significantly through taxes and transfers, in the US the rate goes down only 1.9% to 20.4% after families receive all forms of cash income plus food stamps and other benefits and pay their taxes (if any). Direct comparison of income and poverty across a wide range of countries was made possible by the Luxembourg Income Study (LIS) database.

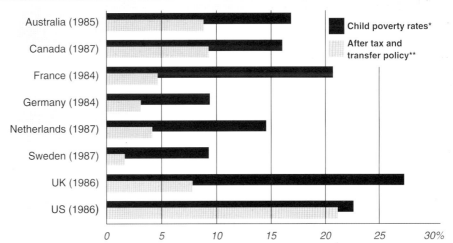

Poverty rates measured as percentages of children living below 40% of the adjusted median family income in each country.

*The ratio of the US poverty line for a three-person family to the adjusted median income was 40% in 1986. Thus, the 40% line is close to the official US poverty line.

** Includes all forms of cash in come plus food stamps and similar benefits in other nations, minus federal income and payroll taxes. Income is adjusted using the US poverty line equivalence scale.

Source: Timothy M. Smeeding, 'The War on Poverty: What Worked?' Testimony to the Joint Economic Committee, the United States Congress, 25 September 1991.

INDEX

ADDITIONAL RESOURCES

You might like to contact the following organisations for further information. Due to the increasing cost of postage, many organisations cannot respond to inquiries unless they receive a stamped, addressed envelope.

Action Aid
Hamlyn House
MacDonald Road
Archway
London N19 5PG
Tel: 0171 281 4101
Fax: 0171 281 5146

A charity working with children, families and communities to improve the quality of life in some of the poorest parts of the world.

ATD Fourth World
48 Addington Square
London SE5 7LB
Tel: 0171 703 3231

Barnardo's
Tanners Lane
Barkingside
Ilford
Essex IG6 1QG
Tel: 0181 550 8822
Fax: 0181 551 6870

British Executive Services Overseas
164 Vauxhall Bridge Road
London SW1V 2RB

British Red Cross Society
9 Grosvenor Cresent
London SW1X 7EJ
Tel: 0171 235 5454
Fax: 0171 245 6315

Child Poverty Action Group (CPAG)
1-5 Bath Street
London EC1V 9PY
Tel: 0171 253 3406

Publish *Poverty* magazine.

Christian Aid
Interchurch House
35 Lower Marsh
London SE1 7RL
Tel: 0171 620 4444

Christain Aid is campaigning to persuade banks and politicians to cancel the Third World debt.

EURODAD – European Network on Debt and Development
Avenue de Cortenbergh 62
B1040
Brussels
Belgium

International Reports: Women and Society
P O Box 824
London SE24 9JS
Tel: 0171 277 6187

To alert the public of the knowledge of the inequalities imposed on women.

Low Pay Unit
37-29 Amwell Street
London EC1R 1UN
Tel: 0171 713 7616
Fax: 0171 713 7581

Investigates and publishes on low pay, poverty and related issues.

National Children's Bureau
8 Wakely Street
London EC1V 7QE
Tel: 0171 843 6000
Fax: 071 278 9512

Overseas Development Administration (ODA)
Information Department
94 Victoria Street
London SW1E 5JL
Tel: 0171 9170503
Fax: 0171 917 0021
A wide range of information about the British aid programme, including the annual review of British aid, *British Overseas Aid*, available free.

Oxfam
274 Banbury Road
Oxford OX2 7DZ
Tel: 01865 311 311

Produces a wide range of publications including free leaflets. Ask for their Resources for Schools and Youth Workers catalogue.

Peace Ethics Animals and Consistant Human Rights (PEACH)
88 Cobden Street
Luton
Beds LU2 0NG
Tel: 01582 459943

Opposes violations of the right to life by war and poverty.

Save the Children
17 Grove Lane
London SE5 8RD
Tel: 0171 703 5400
Fax: 0171 703 2278

Produces a wide range of materials. Ask for their catalogue.

UNICEF
55 Lincoln's Inn Fields
London WC2A 3NB
Tel: 0171 405 5592
Fax: 0171 405 2332

Produces the leaflet *Child Poverty in Rich Nations*.

United Nations Association
3 Whitehall Court
London SW1A 2EL
Tel: 0171 930 2931
Fax: 0171 930 5893

World Development Movement
25 Beehive Place
London SW9 7QR
Tel: 0171 737 6215
Fax: 0171 274 8232

Campaigns for policy changes which directly benefit poor people in the Third World.

World Vision
World Vision House
599 Avebury Boulevard
Central Milton Keynes MK9 3PG
Tel: 01908 841000
Fax: 01908 841001
Produces the magazine 'World Vision'.

ACKNOWLEDGEMENTS

The publisher is grateful for permission to reproduce the following material.

Chapter One: Poverty in the UK

Families, poverty and resources, © International Year of the Family 1994, *Family cost, income and poverty*, © NCH Action for Children, 1995, *Groups vulnerable to poverty*, © Glasgow Caladonian University / Child Resource Unit, Save the Children – Scotland, *Back to the future*, © The New Review, March/April 1995, Ministers launch drive to rebut Rowntree claim of growing inequality, © The Guardian, February 1995, *Exposed; the myth of poverty today*, © The Daily Mail, May 1995, UK accused of failing duty to poor, © The Independent, March 1995, *Family poverty*, © Glasgow Caladonian University / Child Resource Unit, Save the Children – Scotland, *Suggestion for tackling poverty*, Joseph Rowntree Foundation, *Where do you draw the poverty line?*, © Oxfam, Winter 1994/5, *It's enough to make you sick*, © Save the Children, Spring 1993, *Where income support falls short*, © Young People Now, March 1995, *Child and family Poverty in Scotland – the facts*, © Glasgow Caladonian University / Child Resource Unit, Save the Children – Scotland, *Poverty is a war against children*, © Save the Children, *A third of UK children living in poverty*, © Young People Now, March 1995, *Lifes a struggle but a happy struggle*, The Sunday Telegraph Plc, London 1995.

Chapter Two: A Global view

The state of world poverty, © World Development Movement, February 1995, *Poverty summit promises little*, © Christian Aid News, April/June 1995, World faces 'health catastrophe', © The Independent, May 1995, *Famine myths – setting the record straight*, © Save the Children, 1993, *Simply making the food go around*, © New Internationalist, May 1995, *Hunger – the facts*, © New Internationalist, May 1995, *Rooting out poverty*, © ACTIONAID, June 1994, *Women and poverty*, © Women's National Commission, *Poor nations shame rich in UNICEF rankings*, © The Guardian, June 1995, *Child neglect in rich nations*, © Reproduced with the permission of the UK Committee for UNICEF.

Photographs and Illustrations

Pages 5, 12: Anthony Haythornthwaite/Folio Collective, page 6: Crispin Hughes/Photofusion, pages 7, 18: Andrew Smith/Folio Collective, pages 8, 16: Ken Pyne, Pages 14, 20 34: Emma Dodd/Folio Collective, page 21: Sarah Errington/Panos Pictures, page 25: Betty Press/Panos Pictures, page 27: David Dahmen/Panos Pictures, page 28: Sean Sprague/ Panos Pictures, page 29: Jeremy Hartley/Panos Pictures, page 30: Heldun Netocny/Panos Pictures, page 33: Adrian Arbib/ACTIONAID, page 36: UNICEF.

Craig Donnellan
Cambridge
September, 1995